We the People

The American Ways Series

General Editor:
John David Smith
Charles H. Stone Distinguished Professor of American History
University of North Carolina at Charlotte

From the long arcs of America's history, to the short timeframes that convey larger stories, American Ways provides concise, accessible topical histories informed by the latest scholarship and written by scholars who are both leading experts in their fields and polished writers. Books in the series provide general readers and students with compelling introductions to America's social, cultural, political and economic history, underscoring questions of class, gender, racial, and sectional diversity and inclusivity. The titles suggest the multiple ways that the past informs the present and shapes the future in often unforeseen ways.

Current Titles in the Series

How America Eats: A Social History of U.S. Food and Culture, by Jennifer Jensen Wallach
Popular Justice: A History of Lynching in America, by Manfred Berg
Bounds of Their Habitation: Race and Religion in American History, by Paul Harvey
National Pastime: U.S. History through Baseball, by Martin C. Babicz and Thomas W. Zeiler
This Green and Growing Land: Environmental Activism in American History, by Kevin C. Armitage
Wartime America: The World War II Home Front, Second Edition, by John W. Jeffries
Enemies of the State: The Radical Right in America from FDR to Trump, by D. J. Mulloy
Hard Times: Economic Depressions in America, by Richard Striner
We the People: The 500-Year Battle Over Who Is American, by Ben Railton
Litigation Nation: How Lawsuits Represent Changing Ideas of Self, Business Practices, and Right and Wrong in American History, by Peter Charles Hoffer

We the People

The 500-Year Battle Over Who Is American

Ben Railton

ROWMAN & LITTLEFIELD
Lanham • Boulder • New York • London

Published by Rowman & Littlefield
An imprint of The Rowman & Littlefield Publishing Group, Inc.
4501 Forbes Boulevard, Suite 200, Lanham, Maryland 20706
www.rowman.com

6 Tinworth Street, London SE11 5AL

British Library Cataloguing in Publication Information Available

Library of Congress Cataloging-in-Publication Data

Names: Railton, Ben, 1977- author.
Title: We the people : the 500-year battle over who is American / Ben Railton.
Description: Lanham : Rowman & Littlefield, [2019] | Series: The American ways series | Includes
    bibliographical references and index.
Identifiers: LCCN 2019007563| ISBN 9781538128541 (cloth : alk. paper) | ISBN 9781538128558
    (electronic)
Subjects: LCSH: United States—Ethnic relations—History. | United
States—Race relations—History. | National characteristics,
American—History. | Social integration—United States—History.
Classification: LCC E184.A1 R337 2019 | DDC 305.800973—dc23 LC record available at https://
    lccn.loc.gov/2019007563
LC record available at

∞ ™ The paper used in this publication meets the minimum requirements of American National Standard for Information Sciences Permanence of Paper for Printed Library Materials, ANSI/NISO Z39.48-1992.

Contents

Acknowledgments

As has been the case with every project of mine, this book's development itself reflects the benefits of the diverse, inclusive communities in which I'm so fortunate to live and work. At Fitchburg State University, both a Harrod Lecture and a Community Read talk helped me refine these ideas, as did conversations with Prince Addo, Seferine Baez, Chola Chisunka, Katy Covino, Lisa Gim, Michael Hoberman, Ben Lieberman, Irene Martyniuk, Joseph Moser, John Pino, Mitchell Richardson, Diego Ubiera, and Heather Urbanski. For other opportunities to talk about the project, I'm grateful to Karen Peck and the Adult Learning in the Fitchburg Area program; Gail Hoar and her New Hampshire discussion group; Marion Knoll and the Gardner Museum; Rose Sadler, Jeremy Nesoff, and the folks at Facing History and Ourselves; Joan McClymer and the Southgate Women's Circle Breakfast; and Avi Bernstein and the folks at the Brandeis Osher Lifelong Learning Institute. I also learned a lot from my colleagues at both the Northeast MLA and the New England American Studies Association; thanks especially to Hilda Chacón, John Casey Jr., and Maria DiFrancesco at NeMLA, and to Nancy Caronia, Luke Dietrich, and Jonathan Silverman at NEASA. The #Twitterstorians community has been a constant source of feedback, conversation, and inspiration. And thanks as ever to Jeff Renye for his ideas and his friendship.

My blog and my other online writing gigs have been instrumental in helping me develop both the ideas and voice for this project. Thanks especially to Jennifer Bortel and the *Saturday Evening Post* for my current and favorite such gig; thanks as well to Heather Cox Richardson and *We're History*, the *Activist History Review*, Made by History at the *Washington Post*, *Talking Points Memo*, *HuffPost*, *The Conversation*, the American Writers Museum blog, *Democracy Journal*, *The American Prospect*, *Fortune*, and

Ethos Review. For vital support and advice on all things writing, thanks especially to Cecelia Cancellaro and Word Literary, and to Avi Green, Shira Rascoe, Dominik Doemer, and all my colleagues at the Scholars Strategy Network. Jon Sisk, John David Smith, and Kate Powers have made my second experience with Rowman & Littlefield as positive as it has been productive.

Ilene and Steve Railton remain my first and best readers and conversation partners, and Kate Smith has become a new favorite, but with this project, I was also able to share the ideas and work with Aidan and Kyle Railton in a particularly full and meaningful way, and to hear their voices and perspectives, which as always make mine infinitely stronger and better. No one and nothing make me more committed to fighting for the inclusive, inspiring, ideal visions of the American identity, community, and future that they exemplify.

Introduction

The Battle over Who Is an American

"We the People of the United States." That famous phrase which opens the
Constitution's Preamble could not be clearer, both at communicating a national identity and community and at basing the nation's system of government and laws on them.

Yet "we" is an ambiguous pronoun, one that can be used differently in
reference to the same collective group or gathering. If a sporting event is
rained out, the pronoun in the statement "we couldn't play the game today"
would refer equally to both teams in this shared experience. But if that phrase
were to be followed by "hopefully we'll win tomorrow," the speaker would
clearly be using the same pronoun to describe only one of the teams involved, in overt opposition to the other team.

It is my contention in this book that the American "we" has consistently
moved between those two poles. An exclusionary one, where the "we" is
defined as one particular national community and contrasted with groups that
are not part of it (who thus become "thems"), and an inclusive one, where all
those groups are instead part of the "we" and the community it invokes. The
battle between those exclusionary and inclusive definitions, those opposed
but coexisting visions of who is an American, has been central to the nation
since its origin points and has reemerged with particular force and clarity in
our present moment.

From his rise to national political prominence as a leading voice of the
Birther movement in 2011 and 2012, through his June 2015 presidential
campaign announcement that opened with an extended attack on Mexican
immigrants, the January 2017 Muslim ban executive order with which he
began his presidency (and for three versions of which he has fought through

numerous legal challenges), and his October 2018 self-identification as a "nationalist" (among many other moments, statements, and actions), Donald Trump has consistently made an exclusionary definition of American identity central to his political ideas and agenda. This exclusionary vision likewise underlies and helps explain a number of late 2018 Trump controversies: from his description of asylum-seeking refugees as an "invasion" and his concurrent plan to use the military to "close the border"; to his re-Tweeting of a supporter's argument that, "If you weren't born in the United States, you should receive $0 [in federal] assistance"; to his beliefs, stated repeatedly at rallies ahead of the midterm elections, that African American Senate candidate Mike Espy "doesn't fit" in his native Mississippi and that African American gubernatorial candidate Stacey Abrams's "past" made her "unqualified" to be Georgia's governor.

In advancing this consistently exclusionary vision, Trump has capitalized on and extended the decade-long backlash to his predecessor Barack Obama, a figure whose heritage and identity embody an inclusive America and whose opposition attacked him with Birther narratives of his "foreign" background, conspiracy theories about his secret allegiance to Islam, and the telling phrase, "I want my country back!" Throughout his own first presidential campaign, Obama faced such exclusionary definitions of his identity, including an October 2008 *Time* cover story entitled, "Is Barack Obama American Enough?" In response to those exclusionary narratives, Obama offered an inclusive vision of his identity and story as profoundly American, as in his March 2008 "More Perfect Union" speech at Philadelphia's Constitution Center. Obama began that speech by referencing the nation's 1787 founding, going on to link that national identity to his familial and personal ones, and noting, of his multicultural ancestors, "These people are a part of me. And they are part of America, this country that I love."

These two most recent American presidents thus exemplify the inclusive and exclusionary visions of America and reflect the continued battle between representatives and advocates of these narratives over who is an American. Moreover, these interconnected twenty-first-century contexts remind us that the exclusionary and inclusive definitions of American identity have consistently coexisted: that they have been found in the same moments and histories, the same figures and stories, the same ideas and debates. One of the most famous, shared, and longstanding images of American identity, the concept of the nation as a "melting pot," helps illustrate that complex coexistence of exclusion and inclusion.

In his essay "Democracy vs. the Melting Pot," which first appeared in two parts in the February 18 and 25, 1915, editions of the magazine *The Nation*, the prominent cultural critic Horace Kallen highlighted the ways in which the melting pot metaphor had been used to create an exclusionary definition of

American national identity. In this vision of America, Kallen argued, the foundational and ideal "American" was defined by a particular, narrow cultural identity: "They were possessed of ethnic and cultural unity; they were homogenous with respect to ancestry and ideals." And since that ethnic and cultural unity and homogeneity were the desired endpoints of this version of the "melting" process, then that process itself was likewise driven by a very particular set of cultural changes and goals:

> The general notion, "Americanization," appears to denote the adoption of English speech, of American clothes and manners, of the American attitude in politics. It connotes the fusion of the various bloods, and a transmutation by "the miracle of assimilation" of Jews, Slavs, Poles, Frenchmen, Germans, Hindus, Scandinavians into beings similar in background, tradition, outlook, and spirit to the descendants of the British colonists, the Anglo-Saxon stock. (*The Nation* no. 2590, 18–25 February 1915: 191.)

To put it simply, the purpose of this version of the melting pot process was to turn all non-Anglo Americans into close approximations of Anglo Americans, a group that in this version was equated with American identity itself.

This narrative of Americanization and the melting pot did not in and of itself entirely exclude those non–Anglo Americans from becoming part of the nation, of course—not if they could complete that "miracle of assimilation" and become more like Anglo-like on all those levels of identity. Yet at the same time, this melting pot metaphor certainly relied on a definition of America that equated the nation with that "Anglo-Saxon stock," and thus one that excluded any and all other ethnic or national cultures and communities from making up an equal or equally central part of our national identity. Despite his overarching critique of that idea, Kallen himself unintentionally reinforces it at times in the quoted section of the essay, by using the word American (without scare-quotes or any other suggestion that he intends there to complicate this idea) as a shorthand stand-in for Anglo American in phrases like "American clothes and manners." In the best-case scenario, then, this version of the melting pot metaphor equated "American" with "Anglo-Saxon stock," with "the descendants of the British colonists," so fully and successfully that even its critics had a hard time undermining the link.

Moreover, the best-case scenario for this exclusionary definition of American identity was not the one that became dominant in the decade after Kallen's essay. Instead, cultural and social fears of immigrants and non-Anglo cultures (among other forces) drove the moves toward the 1921 and 1924 Quota Acts, the nation's first sweeping immigration laws and ones that were created explicitly to exclude certain ethnic and national cultures and communities and privilege others (especially Anglo Americans and other Northern Europeans). As South Carolina senator Ellison DuRant Smith put it, in a Senate speech defending the 1924 law, "It seems to me the point as to this measure—and I have been so impressed for several years—is that the time has arrived when we should shut the door. . . . Thank God we have in America perhaps the largest percentage of any country in the world of the pure, unadulterated Anglo-Saxon stock, . . . and it is for the preservation of that splendid stock that has characterized us that I would make this not an asylum for the oppressed of all countries, but a country to assimilate and perfect that splendid type of manhood."

Four years later, Texas congressman John Box, arguing in a speech to the House of Representatives for extending the 1924 Quota Act to Mexican arrivals and others from Latin America (many of whom were initially exempt from the laws), made that law's exclusionary underpinnings even clearer still. Since the "purpose of the immigration laws is the protection of American racial stock from further degradation or change through mongrel-ization," Box noted, "every reason which calls for the exclusion of the most wretched, ignorant, dirty, diseased, and degraded people of Europe or Asia demands that the illiterate, unclean, peonized masses moving this way from Mexico be stopped at the border." And Box likewise linked these xenophobic images to exclusionary attitudes toward minority communities already in America, arguing, "This blend of low-grade Spaniard, peonized Indian, and Negro slave mixes with Negroes, mulattoes, and other mongrels, and some sorry whites, already here. The prevention of such mongrelization and the degradation it causes is one of the purposes of our laws which the admission of these people will tend to defeat."

In Smith's and Box's xenophobic and white supremacist remarks we see the logical exclusionary endpoint of defining what "has characterized us" as "pure, unadulterated Anglo-Saxon stock." For in truth, no amount of assimi-lation, miraculous or otherwise, could ever make members of any of the ethnic and national cultures referenced in Kallen's quote, nor others such as Native Americans, African Americans, Asian Americans, Muslim Americans, and many more, into descendants or representatives of that An-glo American ancestry and culture. To define the melting pot as a process of transforming members of such disparate cultures and communities into an Anglo version of American identity was to create from the outset at best a partial and limited, at worst a failed and impossible, and in any case an exclusionary narrative of a unified national community.

Fortunately, that's not the only possible version of the melting pot metaphor, nor, indeed, was it the originating one. As first articulated by a French immi-grant (by way of Canada) who had fought against the English during the French and Indian War, moved to the colonies and owned a farm in upstate New York, and been imprisoned as a spy during the Revolution (among other complex and tellingly American life stages and transformations), the original vision of the melting pot defined it far more inclusively than the one that evolved over time into the subject of Kallen's critiques. This foundational melting pot image represented a process shared by all Americans, one that linked all cultures and communities through a unifying set of transformations and moves toward a genuinely new, inclusive national identity.

Michel Guillaume Jean de Crèvecoeur was born in the Normandy region of France in 1735, and immigrated to the Canadian colony of New France at the age of twenty. Shortly thereafter he joined the French Colonial Militia as a surveyor, and saw action during the French and Indian War, achieving the rank of lieutenant before the war's end. When the French lost the crucial city of Québec to the English in 1759, he chose to leave the militia and immigrate to New York State, where he became a naturalized English citizen under the name of John Hector St. John de Crèvecoeur. He worked as a surveyor and mapmaker until 1770, when he married Mehitable Tippet (the daughter of a wealthy New York merchant) and bought a farm in Orange County. While starting a family and working that farm, he began to write down his observations on American society and culture, wondering, as he would write in his book's Dedication, "Why, though an American, should not I be permitted to share in that extensive intellectual consanguinity" of writers and philosophers "throughout the world?"

In 1779, de Crèvecoeur, already distressed by the uncertainties and dangers of the unfolding American Revolution, learned that his father was ailing and traveled to English-occupied New York City to seek passage back to France. While in the city he was imprisoned by the English for three months as a suspected American spy, but finally allowed to sail for England. In first London and then his childhood home in Normandy he completed work on his manuscript, now a collection of essays entitled *Letters from an American Farmer*, and published it with a London press in 1782. Over a tumultuous next few years spent between France and New York, a period that encompassed the end of the Revolution, Mehitable's death, and the destruction of their farm, de Crèvecoeur would nonetheless revise and expand that book, publishing a two-volume edition in 1784 and a three-volume one in 1787. It was a great success, with translations into French and other European languages, and for the rest of his transatlantic life (he spent many years in New York City, served as a French consul to the new United States government, and died in France in 1813) de Crèvecoeur would frequently be publicly identified with "James," the book's pseudonymous narrator.

The twelve letters in the original *Letters from an American Farmer* cover a great deal of ground, including naturalistic descriptions of flora and fauna, sociological engagements with issues such as slavery and the treatment of Native Americans, and a five-letter sequence on the unique societies of Nantucket and Martha's Vineyard. Yet by far the most famous and influential is Letter III, "What is an American?," which offers one of the first extended descriptions and analyses of what constitutes a uniquely "American" identity. De Crèvecoeur covers a number of subtopics within that frame, but at the letter's heart is the first known metaphor of Americanization as a process of melting:

> He is an American, who leaving behind him all his ancient prejudices and manners, receives new ones from the new mode of life he has embraced, the new government he obeys, and the new rank he holds. . . . Here individuals of all nations are melted into a new race of men, whose labors and posterity will one day cause great changes in the world.

The basic frame of this melting process might seem similar to the one described by Kallen, but it differs from that Anglo-centric and exclusionary version in two key, inclusive ways. For one thing, the desired endpoint here is not an Anglo-like cultural identity, but rather "a new race of men," a shared culture that will be unlike any of those prior ones (or perhaps like a combination of all of them—de Crèvecoeur, like many observers and writers since, has a difficult time pinning down exactly what constitutes this new American culture). And for another, interconnected thing, this version of the melting process, is thus required of every American, and includes "individuals of all nations" (Anglo Americans among the rest) who experience the same shifts and transformations en route to that new American identity. While de Crèvecoeur mostly uses European individuals and cultures as his examples in this letter, his thoughtful and somewhat progressive engagements elsewhere in the book with African American and Native American communities reflect a genuinely and broadly inclusive vision of this new American community, one that can indeed feature "individuals of all nations." Whatever else this inclusive definition of America might entail, it has at its heart a shared experience of transformation that connects, essentially and equally, every person and culture within the national community.

The distinction between Kallen's exclusionary and de Crèvecoeur's inclusive version of the melting pot narrative comprises far more than simply a gap in perspectives on this particular national metaphor, or even on such significant overarching processes as immigration and assimilation. These two contrasting visions succinctly embody more exclusionary and more inclusive definitions of American identity. Exclusionary definitions create a specific American "us," both by equating that "us" with a particular culture (often, as in Smith's remarks, Anglo American, and nearly always European American) and by locating other ethnic and national cultures (most if not all of them present in America as well) outside of that central community. The less thoroughly discriminatory or xenophobic exclusionary definitions do allow, as we see in Kallen's narrative of the melting pot, for the possibility that members of those other cultures can become part of the "American" community, although they can generally do so only by becoming more like the defining culture (and, at least implicitly and often explicitly, less like their own). And lurking beneath even those more flexible exclusionary definitions are the kinds of white supremacist ideas that produced the 1920s Quota Acts and that exemplify the exclusionary definition at its most extreme.

Inclusive definitions, on the other hand, define the American "us" as one which includes all of those cultures present within the national community. The question of what that collection and combination of cultures adds up to has often been as uncertain or ambiguous as it was in de Crèvecoeur's letter, since the inclusive definition is by its nature less focused on any particular elements or factors as distinctly "American." At times inclusive definitions have highlighted national ideals or laws—freedom of speech, religious freedom, social mobility, and other components of what has sometimes been called America's "civic religion"—as providing those shared, linking elements of our identity, although as we'll see throughout my chapters and focal histories, those ideals and laws have too often served exclusionary rather than inclusive purposes. But in truth, the question of what links all of the cultures present in America is a follow-up to, rather than an integral part of, arguments for an inclusive definition of the nation. It's an important follow-up for us to consider and engage, to be sure, but all the same it's a distinct question from whether we include all those cultures within definitions of our national identity and community. That's the first and most fundamental distinction between an exclusionary definition that equates "American" with certain cultures and an inclusive definition that sees all our cultures as part of the core community.

The two versions of the melting pot likewise reflect another important aspect of exclusionary and inclusive definitions of America: that they have frequently, if not indeed consistently, been present in the same concepts and ideas, the same moments and histories, the same figures and stories. I don't mean to suggest that Ellison DuRant Smith had a secret inclusive side to the exclusionary definition of America he offered on the Senate floor in 1924. But we can't separate his exclusionary vision of immigration and America in that year—or the parallel one offered by the decade's resurgent Ku Klux Klan, which was so dominant at the 1924 Democratic National Convention in New York City that the event was nicknamed the Klanbake—from the inclusive narratives featured in the first two novels by the Polish Jewish immigrant writer Anzia Yezierska, *Salome of the Tenements* (1923) and *Bread Givers* (1925). Or the inclusive portrayal of African and African American identity presented in the groundbreaking Harlem Renaissance anthology *The New Negro: An Interpretation* (1925). Or the 1924 Indian Citizenship Act, through which Congress, after centuries of exclusion, granted citizenship to all Native Americans born in the United States. All of these, and many other exclusionary and inclusive perspectives and events, intersected and battled within a shared historical moment.

Virtually every day over the last few years has offered clear illustrations of how much our own moment likewise features such battles between exclusionary and inclusive definitions of America. I return to contemporary America at length in chapter 8 and the conclusion, so here I will briefly highlight just one telling and tragic example: the May 26, 2017, fatal stabbing on a Portland, Oregon, commuter train of two men (and brutal assault on a third) by a white supremacist terrorist, Jeremy Christian, who had been harassing two teenage girls (one Muslim and one African American) with racial and religious hate speech. That harassment was driven by an exclusionary perspective on American identity, as when (per the girls and other witnesses) Christian ordered the two girls to "get out of his country." In his first court appearance, four days after the stabbings, Christian likewise evoked an exclusionary definition of America to defend his actions, shouting, "Get out if you don't like free speech. You call it terrorism; I call it patriotism. You hear me? Die." Further media investigations have revealed that Christian has a long history of participating in white supremacist rallies and organizations, and that both his harassment of the girls and his attack on the three men thus exemplify an extreme and violent but unfortunately not at all unique expression of the resurgent white supremacist, exclusionary narrative of America that has accompanied and followed the 2016 presidential election.

The victims of Christian's exclusionary terrorism embody alternative, inclusive visions of American community on a number of important levels. There's Taliesin Myrddin Namkai-Meche, one of the two men killed by Christian for coming to the defense of the teenagers, whose final words were, "I want everyone on the train to know that I love them." There's Micah Fletcher, the surviving stabbing victim, who explained his own defense of the girls by noting, "If you live here, move here, or if you want to call this city home, it is your home. And we must protect each other like that is the truth, no matter what the consequences. The Muslim community, especially in Portland, needs to understand that there are a lot of us that are not going to stand by and let anybody . . . scare you into thinking you can't be a part of this town, this city, this community, or this country." And, of course, there are the two girls themselves, sixteen-year-old Destinee Mangum (an African American) and her seventeen-year-old Muslim friend (who as of this writing has remained anonymous but whose hijab was the specific target of Christian's initial attacks), whose identities and presences themselves counter Christian's exclusionary definition of America and remind us of the longstanding and still evolving racial and religious diversity at the heart of the inclusive definition.

On the day I finished this manuscript, America suffered another tragic, violent, and overtly exclusionary attack: the October 27, 2018, murder of eleven congregants (and wounding of many more, including four police officers) at Pittsburgh's Tree of Life synagogue by Robert Bowers, a white supremacist and anti-Semitic domestic terrorist. In social media posts, Bowers linked his planned actions to a profoundly exclusionary conspiracy theory advanced by President Trump: that Jewish Americans such as George Soros are paying immigrants such as the refugees making their way to the United States in the so-called migrant caravan. Bowers also referred to immigrants as "invaders" and focused much of his social media hate on one of America's oldest inclusive civic organizations, the Hebrew Immigrant Aid Society (HIAS, founded in New York City in 1881). Like HIAS, Bowers's victims embodied the ideals of an inclusive American community, including a ninety-seven-year-old Holocaust survivor.

That American community likewise features Jeremy Christian, Robert Bowers, and their fellow white supremacists, of course. That's part of what makes the inclusive definition so much harder to articulate and follow up than its alternative: the inclusive vision seeks to define an America through addition rather than subtraction or division, to remember and envision a national community in which the exclusionary perspective has always been and remains present alongside, and consistently interconnects with the diversity that the inclusive definition seeks to highlight and celebrate. Yet challenging as it may be to grapple with, that's the fundamental truth of America, and the central argument of this book: that it is the presence of both definitions, and more exactly their intersections and battles, that has produced the most longstanding and shared American histories and stories.

In the chapters that follow, I will highlight eight examples of such histories and stories, eight illustrations of the battle between exclusionary and inclusive definitions of America from across the five and a quarter centuries of postcontact American history. In virtually all these cases, the exclusionary histories are currently far better remembered (at least in their broad strokes, if not in the complex details of their specifics) than the inclusive alternatives, which makes it both that much harder to focus on the longstanding legacies of the inclusive definition and yet that much more important for us to add those threads back into our collective memories. As a result, while I begin each chapter with the exclusionary histories, I focus at much greater length on the inclusive alternatives. The eight case studies are these:

1. Conquistadors and Cross-Cultural Communities: Christopher Columbus brought more than just disease, slavery, and genocide to the Americas and their indigenous cultures. As illustrated by a letter from his first voyage back to a Spanish supporter, he also brought an exclu-

sionary vision of this new world, one that defined its potential community as entirely European and portrayed its native cultures as either unimportant or invisible. Yet two other early Spanish arrivals offered far more inclusive visions of the emerging community in the Americas: Bartolomé de las Casas, a young priest whose family fortunes were caught up with those of Columbus but who became a vocal advocate for indigenous peoples and their presence and future; and Alvar Nuñez Cabeza de Vaca, a shipwrecked Spanish naval officer who spent nine years wandering the continent and came away transformed, in both his perspective and identity, into a model for an inclusive American community. De Vaca's identity also interestingly parallels that of one of the first prominent Native American individual lives and stories, the tragic, inspiring, inclusive history of Tisquantum (Squanto).

2. Slaves, Revolutionary Enemies or Exemplars: In a cut paragraph from his draft of the Declaration of Independence, Thomas Jefferson defined slavery as an imposition from the British monarch and expressed the fear that the king was now encouraging those slaves to rise up against the colonists; both perspectives were part of a broader narrative that excluded African American slaves from the Revolutionary project. Yet exemplifying an inclusive alternative narrative was Crispus Attucks, the son of a slave father and a Wampanoag mother, and himself a fugitive slave, who became through his participation and death in the Boston Massacre one of the Revolution's first symbols; and Phillis Wheatley, a Boston slave turned published author who produced poetic arguments for the Revolution that overtly linked that cause to her experiences of slavery. Most telling of all were the Massachusetts slaves Elizabeth Freeman and Quock Walker, who along with abolitionist allies used the language and ideals of the Declaration of Independence and the 1780 Massachusetts Constitution to argue successfully in court for their freedom and set the state on the course to abolition.

3. Indian Removal and Inspiring Resistance: Andrew Jackson's policy of Indian removal depended on a multipart process of first redefining Native Americans as a collective race (doing away with a longstanding federal policy of treating distinct tribes individually) and then excluding them from any vision of the states and nation of which they were a part (treating the rights of a state such as Georgia as both entirely distinct from and wholly superior to its Native American inhabitants). Yet in response to Indian removal, we have the 1830 Cherokee Memorials, collectively authored appeals to Congress which used the language and arguments of the Constitution (among other legal and historical evidence) to make the tribe's case; and the 1833

Mashpee Revolt, in which a Cape Cod tribe successfully petitioned the Massachusetts legislature and courts for their sovereignty over their homeland and community. And we have the writings and speeches of native preacher, orator, and activist William Apess, who crafted the Mashpee's petition; who in "An Indian's Looking-Glass for the White Man" (1833) insists on a vision of American community that includes Native Americans; and who in "Eulogy on King Philip" (1836) goes further still, arguing for the seventeenth-century Wampanoag leader as a revolutionary American patriot akin to George Washington.

4. Mexican Americans Have Never Left: The controversial 1840s Mexican American War, and most especially the 1848 Treaty of Guadalupe Hidalgo with which it concluded, forever altered the identities and trajectories of the Hispanic (first Spanish, and then Mexican) American communities that had been part of the American Southwest and West for well more than a century. Although the treaty promised continuity and citizenship to Mexican Americans, the evolving realities of U.S. law, settlement, squatting, and occupation combined to force many Mexican American homeowners and communities off of their lands and out of our collective national narratives. Yet in the enduring presence of communities such as the South Texas Tejanos and the residents of San Diego's Old Town, in the cultural voices of Mexican American authors like María Amparo Ruiz de Burton and María Cristina Mena, and in early-twentieth-century organizations like the League of United Latin American Citizens (LULAC), Mexican Americans became vital parts of an evolving, inclusive vision of the post-treaty United States.

5. Un-American and Unsuccessful Chinese Exclusions: Throughout the mid-nineteenth century there developed in mainstream American society a cultural narrative of bigotry, paranoia, and fear toward the sizeable and growing Chinese American community. That narrative of the so-called Yellow Peril would produce violent acts such as mass lynchings and the 1871 Chinatown Massacre in Los Angeles; political discriminations such as the exclusion of Asian Americans from the groundbreaking 1870 Naturalization Act; and the first federal immigration policy, the 1882 Chinese Exclusion Act and its aftermaths. Yet inspiring Chinese Americans like Wong Kim Ark and his allies offered legal challenges to these discriminatory policies. And the multipart Chinese American life and career of Yung Wing represents a thoroughly inclusive alternative to the Yellow Peril: from his status as the first Asian American college graduate to his volunteering for the Union Army during the Civil War; his efforts to eradicate the "coolie trade" to his founding of the Hartford (Connecticut) Chinese Educational Mission (CEM); and even his struggles to maintain a Chinese

American identity, family, and community in the Exclusion Act era. Both Yung and the CEM students embodied and worked toward an American society that brought together China and the United States, one also highlighted in the journalism and fiction of the groundbreaking writer Sui Sin Far.

6. Fears and Facts of Filipino America: Building on Philippine War propaganda and culminating in the 1920s and 1930s, racist fears of Filipino Americans—as stealing jobs and opportunities from "Americans," as a source of vice and crime, as threatening miscegenation with European American women—led to both acts of mob violence and a series of anti-Filipino policies and laws, particularly the 1935 Filipino Repatriation Act, which sought overtly to return as many Filipino Americans to the Philippines as possible. Yet such laws ignored two crucial histories: that Filipino Americans were the oldest Asian American community, having settled Louisiana fishing villages in the eighteenth century and (after the 1803 Louisiana Purchase made the region part of the United States) participating in such foundational American events as the War of 1812's Battle of New Orleans; and that it was the ongoing U.S. imperial occupation of the Philippines, which both changed and deepened the relationship between the two nations, leading to groundbreaking early-twentieth-century Filipino American lives and stories. Representing both the darkest sides to anti-Filipino discrimination and those more inclusive sides to the Filipino American community is *America Is in the Heart* (1946), an autobiographical novel by the Filipino immigrant, migrant worker, activist, and poet Carlos Bulosan.

7. Everything Japanese Internment Got Wrong: The Roosevelt administration's policy of Japanese Internment represents one of the most explicitly exclusionary moments in our history, defining (in the infamous 1942 Executive Order 9066) internment's goals as both "prescribing regulations for the conduct and control of alien enemies" and "designating areas . . . from which any or all persons may be excluded." Japanese Americans such as Fred Korematsu and Mitsuye Endo resisted internment through inspiring, inclusive legal challenges. And when, in response to Japanese American patriotic volunteers, the U.S. military changed its policy to allow for Japanese American soldiers, tens of thousands of men immediately volunteered to serve, including many from the internment camps. By the war's end, more than 33,000 Japanese Americans had served as part of two battalions; of one, the legendary "Purple Heart Battalion," General George Marshall noted that "they showed rare courage and tremendous fighting spirit. Everybody wanted them." These internment-era inclusive alter-

natives have been echoed by the subsequent, activist American lives and efforts of detainees such as Yuri Kochiyama and George Takei.

8. There's Nothing New about Muslim Americans: Even before the 2017 executive orders that have created anti-Muslim travel bans and refugee restrictions, the twenty-first-century's exclusionary national narratives have targeted Muslim Americans more than any other cultural or religious group. While each hate crime, immigration restriction, or surveillance policy has been framed through specific, contemporary lenses of terrorism and national security, all of these debates ignore the longstanding and multi-faceted history of Muslim American communities. That history extends back to the substantial portion of slaves who were Muslim; deepens significantly during the American Revolution, when the Charleston, South Carolina, Moroccan (or "Moorish") American community directly influenced key laws on religion and citizenship; and includes numerous Muslim American communities and figures across the nation in the early twentieth century, such as the truly unique yet still telling life and career of Montana's Hot Tamale Louie (the Afghani immigrant Tarif Khan). Only by better remembering these historical Muslim Americans can we envision an inclusive twenty-first-century national identity that accurately locates Muslim Americans as an integral part of, rather than a threat to, the nation's present and future.

While the twenty-first century echoes and extensions of those Muslim American exclusionary and inclusive histories are particularly clear, I would argue that each of these eight moments and histories resonates fully and potently with continuing issues and debates in our contemporary society and culture. In the conclusion I draw out some of those numerous contemporary connections, and make the case for why our twenty-first-century moment represents not only another period of intense battle between exclusionary and inclusive visions, but also, and in a new and crucial way, an amplification of that conflict. That is, for a variety of reasons—such as the presence and power of public scholarly voices, organizations, and activist movements such as #FergusonSyllabus, many of them directly opposed to other public historical efforts such as Dinesh D'Souza's books and films; prominent and divisive debates over public historical and cultural topics such as Confederate memorials and Native American reservations; and the Trump administration and the contested meanings of slogans such as "Make America Great Again" and "America First"—our moment features, alongside its own pivotal battles between exclusionary and inclusive definitions of American identity, a heightened awareness of the historical and national origins, legacies, and stakes of those defining battles.

Yet if those twenty-first-century connections frame my book, the chapters' specific histories and stories are at its center. For one thing, and as is so often the case, our current debates are limited and incomplete because of how little we remember those histories—and better remembering them requires us to focus on them first and foremost on their own terms, rather than simply making them into prehistories of our own moment and issues. As a result, in the course of these chapters I focus on narrating their respective moments and histories, figures and stories, working to capture both the darker and more exclusionary and (especially) the more inspiring and inclusive sides to each. Las Casas and de Vaca, Elizabeth Freeman and Quock Walker, William Apess and the Mashpee Revolt, Yung Wing and the Chinese Educational Mission, and all of these figures and stories are quite simply some of the most interesting and powerful in American history, and yet are all largely left out of our collective memories and national narratives. Sharing those figures, stories, and histories is a worthwhile and significant goal, and if my chapters inspire further research and reading into them and their respective periods, I'll have accomplished a great deal.

For another, and final, introductory thing, each and every one of these histories and stories features and embodies the exclusionary and inclusive definitions of America far more clearly and cogently than any broad or theoretical scholarly account could ever hope to. Partly that's due to the power of storytelling: in my last book, *History and Hope in American Literature: Models of Critical Patriotism* (Rowman & Littlefield, 2016), I made the case for how novels and other works of creative literature can help us better remember our histories. And while the stories in *We the People: The 500-Year Battle over Who Is American* are all true, they're just as compelling and moving as the best literary or cultural works, and engage our attention and understanding quite effectively as a result. And partly it's a reminder of one of the most consistent and consistently inspiring threads in American history: the ability of amazing individuals, supported by allies and communities, to resist the darkest and most exclusionary moments in both their lives and our society, and to model instead, courageously and patriotically, the most inclusive and ideal images of America. I'll end this introduction with a brief story of one such individual and moment that I couldn't fit into any of the chapters.

In 1892, having just turned thirty years old, the African American journalist, editor, and anti-lynching activist Ida B. Wells experienced precisely such a profound personal and civic turning point. The early 1890s are considered by historians to be the nadir of the lynching epidemic (which stretched from the 1860s through the 1960s), and in March 1892 that epidemic hit Wells very close to home. Three of her Memphis friends, successful store-owner Thomas Moss and two fellow African Americans (Calvin McDowell and Will Stewart), were lynched after defending Moss's store, the People's Grocery, from a white mob. When Wells covered the lynching in her newspaper, the *Memphis Free Speech*, taking the occasion to detail the contexts and realities behind lynching's propagandistic myths (of African American criminality, rape, and social degeneracy), rampaging whites destroyed the newspaper's offices while she was on an overseas speaking tour and warned her not to return to Memphis or continue her efforts, at quite explicit penalty of death.

No one could have blamed Wells if she backed down or at least took a break from her most vocal anti-lynching activism, but instead she did precisely the opposite: upon returning to New York City from abroad, she immediately published her first book, *Southern Horrors: Lynch Law in All Its Phases* (1892), with a New York press and set about distributing it as widely as possible. This darkest moment in Wells's life marked, to put it simply, the starting point for her moves toward a fully national presence and voice, one that would never be silenced. Having come face to face with the most violent and exclusionary elements of her nation, Wells fought back, destroying the myths and fallacies underpinning that exclusionary narrative and modeling in its place an inclusive definition, one in which her voice and community had vital roles to play in moving the nation toward a more perfect union. That nation has always featured a battle between exclusionary and inclusive definitions, and perhaps always will—but the more we remember those histories, the more stories like Wells's, and all those of my focal figures, can inspire us to fight for an inclusive America.

Chapter One

Conquistadors and
Cross-Cultural Communities

The horrors and tragedies for indigenous peoples that followed Christopher Columbus's four voyages to the Americas are well known. Some of them, particularly the diseases such as smallpox and influenza to which the Europeans had become relatively inoculated but which were entirely new and devastating for the indigenous cultures, were tragic accidents of history. But most of the horrors were far more intentional: the genocide and cultural destruction that the Europeans visited upon the natives in order to pave the way for their colonies and empires and the enslavement of millions of natives that served as a primary resource for those colonial and imperial enterprises.

Nor were those horrors simply effects or aftermaths of European exploration in the Americas. As Columbus's journals and letters reveal, he began considering conquering and enslaving the indigenous peoples from his first 1492 encounters with them, taking native prisoners on his first voyage and sending them back to Spain to investigate precisely those possibilities. Moreover, those documents illustrate the crucial underlying perspective that allowed Columbus to think of and treat the indigenous peoples in those ways: an exclusionary vision of this new world he had "discovered," an imagination of future European colonization of what he called "the Indies" that had no place for its native cultures as anything other than obstacles to be overcome or slaves to be exploited.

One particular Columbus text from his first voyage, his February 1493 letter to Luis de Santángel, exemplifies that exclusionary perspective on the Americas and its peoples. Santángel, the finance minister to Spain's King Ferdinand II, had been Columbus's strongest and most consistent backer at the Spanish court, convincing the initially reluctant Ferdinand and his wife, Queen Isabella, to support the voyage and then providing most of its funding (including a good deal from his own resources). As such, he was an especially important audience for Columbus's initial reflections on the places and cultures he encountered on that first voyage, reflections that Columbus crafted carefully in the February 1493 letter for both that meaningful individual reader and the broader European community he represented.

Columbus's central goal in that letter was to portray these newly "discovered" islands as ripe and ready for European colonization. It's to that end, for example, that he calls the islands "most fertile to an excessive degree" and their mountains "most lofty," yet somehow at the same time "all accessible" (Columbus writes the letter in his adopted language of Spanish; I am relying on the translation in the *Norton Anthology of American Literature* for these quotes). He makes clear that this new world offers something distinct from any setting previously familiar to his Spanish and European audiences, writing of the "many havens on the sea-coast, incomparable with any others that I know of in Christendom." And he consistently imagines what future European arrivals can and will do in and with this place, as when he describes "the soil" as "so beautiful and rich for planting and sowing, for breeding cattle of all sorts, for building of towns and villages."

The building of those towns and villages faced a clear difficulty, however: the "innumerable small villages and numberless population" that Columbus's explorations of the islands had encountered. Yet in the same sentence as that quote Columbus notes that his men had found "nothing of importance," and it's precisely by depicting the indigenous cultures as insignificant, and thus as a nonexistent part of the future world he imagines in this place, that Columbus can envision colonization. In the letter's first two sentences he writes that he has "found very many islands peopled with inhabitants beyond number. And of them all, I have taken possession for their Highnesses, with proclamation and the royal standard displayed; and I was not gainsaid." The fact that "them all" could refer to either the islands or their indigenous inhabitants is exactly the point: in this letter and exclusionary perspective, those innumerable inhabitants in no way interfere with either Columbus's ability to take possession or the future use to which Spain might put these colonial possessions.

It is in his immediate renaming of the islands that Columbus most fully displays this exclusionary perspective on the Americas. He lists all the new names in the letter's opening paragraph, but the first sentence in that section is the most telling: "To the first which I found, I gave the name Saint Salvador, in commemoration of His High Majesty, who marvelously hath given all this; the Indians call it Guanahani." Columbus knows full well that the island already has a name, likely because, "As soon as I arrived in the Indies, in the first island that I found, I took some of [the natives] by force, to the intent that they should learn our speech and give me information." But compared to information about fertile soil and accessible harbors, the native name for the island is both useless and meaningless to Columbus and his Spanish audience, will have no place in the European future he's already begun imagining for this place.

That future and perspective are summed up in one sentence from this illustrative letter: "Española is a marvel." "Española" was Columbus's new name for one particular island (later modified to Hispañiola, still the name for the island on which Haiti and the Dominican Republic are located), but I would argue that it was also a great deal more than that. It was a word that captured how much Columbus had immediately and fully defined the Americas (or, in his tellingly mistaken perspective, Indies) as an extension of Spain (España), a site of future European colonization and community. That definition required excluding all the indigenous cultures and inhabitants from that imagined community, and it was that exclusion which truly made the subsequent genocides and enslavements possible.

As those tragic histories reflect, the exclusionary definition held sway far too consistently and destructively throughout the era of European exploration and colonization. Yet there were other figures, both European and indigenous, who saw, experienced, and embodied a different future for the Americas, an inclusive definition in which all these cultures would play a role. The young Spanish priest, with multilayered, multigenerational ties to Columbus and his family, who became an impassioned advocate for the indigenous peoples. The Spanish naval officer whose unique and transformative American journey led him to see both Native Americans and himself in a new light. And the New England Native American who experienced the worst of genocide and slavery but became a cross-cultural translator and mediator between the region's native and European cultures. All of these figures make clear that the battle between exclusionary and inclusive definitions of the Americas has been fought since the first moments of contact.

When Columbus returned to Spain in early 1493, at the end of his successful first voyage, he traveled to many of the country's largest cities to show off all that he had brought back from the Americas, including seven captive indigenous people from the Taino tribe. On March 31, 1493 (Palm Sunday), Columbus paraded through the southern city of Sevilla, where among the thousands of spectators were local merchant Pedro de las Casas and his nine-year-old son Bartolomé. Pedro was so excited by what he saw that he (along with his brother and more than a thousand other men) would join Columbus on his second voyage to the Americas, which departed six months later in September 1493. But it was Pedro's son, young Bartolomé de las Casas, who would go on to become one of the most influential and inclusive European voices of the exploration period.

Over the next decade Bartolomé studied for the priesthood, receiving his first minor orders in February 1502. That same month he departed for

Hispañiola, where he joined his father in running a large *hacienda* (slave plantation), served as a provisioner (provider of supplies) for the Spanish military, and became the island's first ordained priest. If the first and second roles broadly supported Columbus's exclusionary vision for a Spanish new world, in the third las Casas became even more closely tied to the Columbus family: when las Casas traveled to Rome in 1507 to be ordained by the Pope, he took the opportunity to advocate for Columbus's American inheritance. Columbus himself had died in 1506, but las Casas brought Columbus's older brother Bartholomew to meet Pope Julius II, and together they successfully secured that American inheritance for Columbus's son, Diego. In all these ways, las Casas would seem to have embodied Columbus's proposed project for the Americas.

No one incident or factor altered las Casas's perspective on the status of indigenous cultures within that community; instead, a series of such factors accumulated in the young priest's experiences. Besides observing the daily lives and abuses of slaves on a plantation like his father's, in his role as a military provisioner, las Casas traveled the island and witnessed many more such harsh conditions, especially where natives were used to mine for gold. He also accompanied two particularly brutal Spanish expeditions: governor of Hispañiola Nicolás de Ovando's 1503 military expedition across the island, during which Ovando massacred a number of native leaders as a matter of policy; and Pánfilo de Narváez's 1510 exploration of Cuba, during which (as las Casas himself later chronicled) some two thousand natives were murdered without provocation.

Las Casas served as chaplain for the Narváez expedition, and it was precisely the combination of his religious role with his observations of these brutalities that gradually pushed him toward a new perspective. After his 1507 ordination in Rome, las Casas returned to Hispañiola to serve as the island's *doctrinero*, the official catechist for the native population, a role that put him in a very different relationship to indigenous peoples. In 1510, a community of Dominican priests joined the Spanish colony, and in December 1511, one of their leaders, Friar Antón Montesino, delivered an Advent sermon condemning the *encomienda* (the slave system) as a mortal sin. Las Casas, still only twenty-seven-years old at that time, did not immediately respond to Montesino's call to action. But it, like all these accumulated moments and factors, added to his perspective, and in 1514, the dam burst: he renounced his plantations and participation in both the slave and military provisioning systems and began preaching sermons against the encomienda system and in support of the indigenous cultures.

Las Casas would live for fifty-two more years after his epiphany and would dedicate much of that remaining half-century to activism on behalf of the region's indigenous peoples and an inclusive vision of the Americas. Cardinal Ximénez de Cisneros, an early supporter of las Casas's efforts at reform and the Spanish Regent after Ferdinand's 1516 death, gave las Casas the title "Protector of the Indians," and with the help of influential friends like Cisneros, las Casas promoted a wide range of proposals and plans, all designed to reimagine a European community in the Americas that had space for indigenous cultures within it. For example, with Cisneros's support, las Casas proposed to remove all natives from *encomiendas* and settle them in *corregimientos*, or "crown-free towns" that would be self-sustaining indigenous villages. When Cisneros died in 1517 and this plan stalled, las Casas approached the new monarch Charles I with a plan for colonization by farmers rather than soldiers, an experiment that Charles granted las Casas permission to perform in the South American colony of Cumaná (in modern-day Venezuela).

The Cumaná colony failed to live up to las Casas's hopes, as a number of its Spanish settlers turned to slave-owning despite his admonitions. Yet such frustrating failures notwithstanding, las Casas achieved a number of successes both practical and philosophical in his lifelong pursuit of a more inclusive society in and vision of the Americas. Exemplifying the practical successes is his last, achieved in 1564 when he was eighty years old (just two years before his death). A group of Peruvian slave owners offered to purchase indigenous peoples in perpetuity from the Spanish crown for 8 million gold ducats, and King Philip II (weighed down by debt) was ready to accept the offer. Yet thanks to the efforts of las Casas and his allies, arguing for the rights of Peruvian natives to control both their futures and any remaining Incan treasures (without access to which the slave owners would never be able to put together the necessary funds), a royal commission to investigate the offer stalled and the transaction was never completed.

As he so often did, las Casas developed his arguments on behalf of the Peruvian natives in a written text (his last), *Los Tesoros del Perú* (*The Treasures of Peru*, 1564). And it is his most significant written work, *Brevíssima Relación de la Destruición de las Indias* (*Brief Account of the Destruction of the Indies*, 1552), that represents the culmination of las Casas's lifelong philosophical arguments for a more inclusive definition of the Americas. The title alone links the region to its native peoples, connecting the tragic and horrific histories of those indigenous peoples to what las Casas calls, in the book's prologue, "the evil and the harm, the losses and diminutions suffered by those great kingdoms, each so vast and so wonderful that it would be more appropriate to refer to them as the New World of the Americas." That is, from the title on, las Casas portrays the indigenous peoples not as insignificant obstacles to or exploited resources for European colonization but rather as vital American cultures in their own right, communities whose losses across the prior half-century constitute as well losses and diminutions for the region and its future as a whole.

As such, much of the *Brief Account* comprises a record of brutality and horror, a history of "the boldness and the unreason of those who count it as nothing to drench the Americas in human blood and to dispossess the people who are the natural masters and dwellers in those vast and marvelous kingdoms." Yet the word "dispossess" there, so clearly contrasted to the exclusionary perspective that led Columbus to write that he had "taken possession" of both the islands and their inhabitants, reflects how fully and consistently las Casas uses his historical account to create an alternative vision of the Americas. In place of the exclusionary colonial project, he offers an inclusive definition, one in which the indigenous peoples occupy a central role, and it is those Europeans who cannot imagine a shared community and future—those who treat the natives only with dispossession, violence, and enslavement—who are opposed to both nature and reason.

In the book's conclusion, las Casas imagines precisely such an inclusive future, one in which the Spanish king and Holy Roman Emperor Charles V (his intended audience) "put[s] a stop to the wickedness" and "treachery towards the people of the continent," and thus one in which "the teeming millions in the New World . . . do not continue to die in ignorance, but rather are brought to knowledge of God and thereby saved." It's important to be clear that for las Casas this inclusive American community was dependent not only on a shift in European perspectives and policies but also on the conversion of the natives to Christianity; he was a devoted Catholic priest to the end, after all. Yet even that attitude, while certainly troubling in its dismissal of indigenous religions and cultures, reflected las Casas's desire for a community—spiritual as well as social—which the natives and Europeans could occupy together. In response to the horrors and tragedies produced by the exclusionary definition, las Casas imagined and worked tirelessly for such an inclusive alternative.

If las Casas imagined and worked for that inclusive American community, however, it was a fellow Spanish explorer—and a participant in another expedition led by Pánfilo de Narváez, this one ill fated—who personally experienced a unique and strikingly transformative version of that alternative America. In the course of nearly a decade of travels across the North American continent in the aftermath of a shipwreck, Álvar Nuñez Cabeza de Vaca became a complicated but integral part of a number of native cultures, shifting from the role of captive to those of trader, healer, and eventually leader of a multicultural indigenous community. When he returned to Spain, he wrote about both that journey and those native cultures in a 1542 book (addressed to the same Charles V as las Casas's 1552 *Brief Account*) that, like de Vaca himself, embodied this new, inclusive American identity.

De Vaca was born around 1490 in the southwestern Spanish town of Jerez de la Frontera (near the city of Cadiz). He was the descendent of military figures on both his father's and mother's sides, and he enlisted in the army at a young age, serving with distinction in campaigns across Spain and Europe. When King Charles I commissioned Pánfilo de Narváez in 1527 to explore the uncharted territory known as La Florida (modern-day Florida), de Vaca signed on for his first expedition to the Americas, taking on the dual important roles of treasurer and marshal. While de Vaca was not overtly a new world conquistador like Narváez, he was certainly a Spanish military officer and approached his arrival in the Americas entirely through that lens.

In the first section of his *Relación de Álvar Nuñez Cabeza de Vaca* (1542), the portion of the book which details the Narváez expedition up to its disastrous finale, de Vaca captures his initial, exclusionary perspective on the Americas and its indigenous cultures. In his first encounter with natives, he notes that "they made many signs and threatening gestures to us and it seemed to us that they were telling us to leave the land," a sentence as telling in its opposed "they" and "us" pronouns as its specific exchange. When a subsequent encounter turns violent, de Vaca frames it as almost a religious conflict, writing, "They shot at one of our Christians, and God willed that they not wound him." And when the expedition captures a group of natives, de Vaca carries forward each of those attitudes, dismissing what he observes of their spirituality as "a type of idolatry" and then describing at length his interrogation of the natives in an effort to learn where they had acquired the "samples of gold" used in those religious ceremonies. In his own words and perspective as well as his actions, de Vaca, the military officer, did Columbus's exclusionary project proud.

Had the Narváez expedition gone as planned, perhaps de Vaca would have maintained that exclusionary perspective, becoming another brutal European conquistador and returning for multiple expeditions as had Narváez by this time, but it most definitely did not, as a shipwreck broke up the expedition, led to the deaths of Narváez and nearly all of his men, and left de Vaca and a trio of comrades (one of whom the fascinating figure known as Estevanico, a North African Muslim slave turned explorer about whom I write in chapter 8) separated for what would become nearly nine years of wandering across North America (beginning in Florida and ending in western Mexico). In the course of that striking and transformative decade, everything changed for de Vaca, including his perspective. Three quotes from his book that employ the concept of nakedness can sum up three key stages of his shifts in perspective and identity during and after his journey.

Immediately after he and his men are separated from Narváez for good, de Vaca writes that they found themselves "naked as the day we were born," having "lost everything we carried with us. And although all of it was of little value, at that time it was worth a great deal." While it's quite possible that the nakedness de Vaca highlights here was literal, the concept also reflects how fully his perspective and identity had been linked to his roles within the community of the Narváez expedition. Without that European community and identity, he and his comrades will seemingly have to begin anew, a process that at this initial moment is understandably frightening to de Vaca—and that only becomes more so when they are taken captive by the first indigenous peoples they encounter.

Yet captivity is only the first of many roles that de Vaca plays within the numerous indigenous communities among whom he finds himself. In the course of his nine years of wandering, relying on his own ingenuity and knowledge but also on the communal needs, cross-tribal relationships, and hospitality of his hosts, de Vaca becomes a mediator, a trader, and a healer, among other roles. Writing about one portion of the journey, he employs the concept of nakedness in a new way that captures these shifting roles: "Throughout this entire land, we went about naked, and since we were not accustomed to it, like serpents we changed our skins twice a year." Again, the literal meaning of nakedness here (and of peeling and healing skin after extended sun exposure) is complemented and extended by its symbolic side, in this case reflecting how much de Vaca and his men have to constantly adapt to fit into and live with their indigenous communities.

Those nine years of adaptation produce an entirely new perspective, one de Vaca captures in the book's introduction (a letter addressed directly to Charles V) with yet another reference to nakedness. He calls the book "an account of all that I was able to observe and learn in the nine years that I walked lost and naked through many and very strange lands." While it might seem that being lost and naked is a bad thing (as de Vaca certainly felt it to be after the shipwreck), I would argue that the parallel structure of this sentence directly links that state to his ability to observe and learn about (and from) the lands and indigenous cultures of the Americas. Of course that process began accidentally, and its resulting effects and changes were in large part forced. Yet they were changes nonetheless, and changes that allowed de Vaca to both imagine and come to embody a far more inclusive vision of European and indigenous relationships and community.

That shift is reflected most overtly in the book's many extended and nuanced descriptions of the native cultures with which de Vaca and his comrades live. While de Vaca was not necessarily more interested in or sympathetic to the indigenous peoples than was las Casas, de Vaca's immersive experiences with his focal cultures gave him an in-depth understanding that was quite simply not available to las Casas or any other European of the era. As a result, he writes at length about such complex social and psychological subjects as marital dynamics and relationships with in-laws, the individual and communal mourning process after the deaths of parents or children, and the effects of seasonal shifts in available food and resources, among many other topics. He observes and analyzes such subjects with the perspective of an amateur but thoughtful ethnographer, both in his attention to detail and in his general ability to withhold judgments of what he's describing.

Those ethnographic sections of the book treat the continent's indigenous cultures as a large, diverse, and evolving collection of communities, a perspective that would be a prerequisite for imagining a broader American community featuring them as well as European arrivals. Moreover, since de Vaca was himself a European arrival who spent nearly a decade living in precisely such cross-cultural communities, he's able to link his descriptions of native peoples to shared experiences alongside them. Concluding an extended account of the lengths to which one tribe must go to find food in harsh desert conditions, de Vaca writes, "and in this way they satisfy their hunger two or three times a year at as great a cost as I have said. And for having lived through it, I can affirm that no hardship endured in the world equals this one." While de Vaca's use of "they" and "I" defines him as still somewhat outside of the indigenous culture, he has nonetheless lived through and can reflect on the same experiences as they, a mutual hardship that is also a starting point toward an inclusive American community based on such shared experiences and perspectives.

That new, inclusive community is put to the test in the final section of de Vaca's journey and book, when he, his comrades, and the multi-indigenous community now traveling with them hear of a nearby Spanish expedition (led by the conquistador Diego de Alcaraz). This is the first de Vaca has heard of fellow Europeans for nearly a decade and would thus seem to be an occasion for reunion and celebration. Yet de Vaca is instead far more concerned with what this Spanish expedition might mean for the native peoples, and before seeking out the Spanish, he tells his indigenous peers that he is "going to look for the Christians to tell them that they should not kill [the natives] or take them as slaves, nor should they take them out of their lands, nor should they do them any other harm whatsoever." Here de Vaca's language both separates him from the Spanish expedition (he consistently calls them "the Christians" in this section) and links him to the indigenous peoples, with whom he shares both a perspective and a fear of what results the Europeans' exclusionary attitudes might produce.

These exclusionary and inclusive perspectives come into direct conflict when de Vaca's multitribal community encounters the Alcaraz expedition. The Spanish argue that de Vaca and his men remain European, and are thus both subject to Alcaraz's command and unable to lead or influence the indigenous communities: "The Christians . . . made their interpreter tell [the natives] that we were of the same people as they, and that we had been lost for a long time, and that we were people of ill fortune and no worth, and that they were the lords of the land whom the Indians were to serve and obey." Yet in response, the natives define de Vaca and his men, the Alcaraz expedition, and their own relationship to these two communities and cultures very differently:

> But of all this the Indians were only superficially or not at all convinced of what they told them. Rather, some talked with others among themselves, saying that the Christians were lying, because we came from where the sun rose, and they from where it set; and that we cured the sick, and that they killed those who were well; and that we came naked and barefoot, and they went about dressed and on horses and with lances; and that we did not covet anything but rather, everything they gave us we later returned and remained with nothing, and that the others had no other objective but to steal everything they found and did not give anything to anyone. And in this manner, they conveyed everything about us and held it in high esteem to the detriment of the others.

Crucially, what differentiates de Vaca and his men from the Spanish in this multipart comparison are their respective perspectives on the American community of which they and the natives are all now complicatedly a part. To these indigenous people, de Vaca is no longer an exclusionary European; he has become, the natives see and communicate, part of an inclusive community alongside them.

De Vaca did not join the Alcaraz expedition, but not long after this encounter he and his men reached Spanish-held Mexico City, returning to Spain from there in 1537. Over the next few years he would both write and publish his *Relation* (1542) and return to the Americas, this time as an explorer for and then governor of the Río de la Plata colony in South America. In those colonial roles he attempted to implement policies more friendly to the local indigenous cultures, a project that met with the same frustrating resistance from his fellow European settlers as had las Casas's reforms (and which led to de Vaca's permanent return to Spain in the late 1540s). Yet like las Casas, de Vaca imagined and worked toward an American community that could include both European arrivals and indigenous peoples—and in de Vaca's case, he had a decade of immersive, lived experiences that modeled such a community. Taken together, these two sixteenth-century Spaniards offer a vastly distinct, more inclusive perspective on and definition of America than the exclusionary attitudes of Columbus and his conquistador ilk.

Despite their significant differences, however, Columbus, las Casas, and de Vaca were all European, and so represented only a small fraction of the cultures who came together in the Americas during the contact and exploration era. Finding the stories and perspectives of indigenous peoples from that period can be extremely difficult, and finding ones that have not been filtered through the writings and perspectives of European arrivals nearly impossible. Yet while recognizing those limitations, we can and should still seek out such indigenous voices, stories, and histories, and add them to our understanding of the battle to define America in this first postcontact era. In the case of Tisquantum (Squanto), a Patuxet Wampanoag Native American whose story famously intersected with that of the Plymouth Pilgrims in Massachusetts, remembering his life more fully both highlights the horrific effects of the exclusionary histories and models the possibilities and meanings of an inclusive alternative community and America.

Tisquantum's postcontact story (his life before European contact is largely unknown) begins with the all-too-familiar refrain of kidnapping and enslavement. While it is the Spanish conquistadors who are most frequently associated with the practice of enslaving the indigenous peoples, English explorers likewise began to do so within the earliest years of English arrival to the Americas, well before there were English settlements in places like Massachusetts (where Tisquantum's Patuxet tribe resided, on the western coast of what would come to be known as Cape Cod Bay). Explorers such as Captain George Weymouth began kidnapping Massachusetts natives as early as 1605, and over the next decade the practice—or at least the threat, as these English explorers did not have the numbers of men that the Spanish did and so their attempts were less consistently successful—became common. The English were apparently just as willing as their southern European brethren to enact from the outset an exclusionary vision of this newly encountered world and its indigenous cultures.

Tisquantum fell victim to that horrific practice in 1614, when Thomas Hunt, an English explorer traveling with Captain John Smith on his trading expedition to New England, kidnapped twenty-seven local natives and transported them to Spain where he sold them into slavery. The next few years in Tisquantum's life are once again mostly lost to historians, but at some point he made his way to England, from which he was sent as a slave (or perhaps by this time a servant, although in either case he likely had no say in the matter) to a new English colony in Newfoundland. Around 1619, an English member of that colony, Thomas Dermer, brought Tisquantum back to New England, where he learned that the rest of his Patuxet tribe had met a tragic end, destroyed by one of the many epidemics that Europeans brought to the Americas as an accidental complement to their more intentional genocides.

Left without a home or community by European devastations both personal and global, intentional and accidental, Tisquantum went to live with a neighboring Cape Cod tribe, the Pokanoket Wampanoag. At this point, it would have been entirely understandable if he had wanted nothing more to do with Europeans, or even had become overtly hostile to any such further contacts. Yet a year or so later, when the *Mayflower* arrived off of Cape Cod in November 1620 and the Pilgrims settled at nearby Plymouth, quite close to the site of the Patuxet tribe's former summer village, Tisquantum decided instead to take on a potent cross-cultural role. He befriended and aided the English, worked to bring together the English and native cultures (despite suspicions of his motives from both sides), and modeled an inclusive New England and American community in the process.

A number of factors likely played into that surprising decision. Tisquantum's years of slavery and servitude in Europe and Newfoundland had enabled him to learn English (among other languages), and of course had also prepared him to interact with European communities far more easily than most of the period's Native Americans. It's also possible that his position with the Pokanoket was not particularly secure (some historians have even argued that he was treated as a prisoner of the tribe), and that he thus saw the arrival of these European settlers as a chance to prove his value to and make powerful friends within multiple communities. Such a perspective would be understandable and wise for anyone in Tisquantum's position, much less one with years of tragic experiences in his recent past. And in truth, whatever his motivations—and to see them as complex and even contradictory is simply to give him the humanity that the exclusionary definition would deny him— Tisquantum's efforts did indeed prove invaluable both to the English and for an emerging, inclusive New England community overall.

No moment better exemplifies his multilayered contributions to that community than the "First Thanksgiving." While the stereotypical, children's story version of that autumn 1621 event has been often overplayed in our national collective memories, allowing us to forget the much less attractive exclusionary histories of genocide and enslavement, we shouldn't respond by swinging the pendulum too far in the opposite direction and downplaying the moment's significance. For one thing, the Pilgrims had good reason to hold this three-day autumn celebration (it was held sometime between September and November, and they did not call it Thanksgiving): they had brought in a bountiful harvest and were envisioning a far less horrific winter than the first they had spent in Plymouth. In his account of the celebration for an English audience in his book *Mourt's Relation* (1622), Pilgrim Edward Winslow writes, "Although it be not always so plentiful, as it was at this time with us, yet by the goodness of God, we are so far from want, that we often wish you partakers of our plenty." And it was chiefly to Tisquantum, and all that he had taught them of farming and trading in the region, that the Pilgrims owed this crucially plentiful autumn harvest.

For another thing, the Pilgrims hosted honored Wampanoag guests at the celebration. As Winslow describes it, "Many of the Indians [came] amongst us, and amongst the rest their greatest king Massasoit, with some ninety men, whom for three days we entertained and feasted, and they went out and killed five deer, which they brought to the plantation and bestowed on our Governor, and upon the Captain and others." This peaceful, cross-cultural gathering was far from a given, as the Pilgrims' first experiences with the Wampanoag in late 1620 and early 1621 had been far more hostile and exclusionary.

William Bradford, the community's governor at the time of the harvest celebration, describes two such experiences in chapter 10 of his communal history *Of Plymouth Plantation* (written between 1630 and 1651 and published posthumously). When the Pilgrims initially explored Cape Cod, they found a store of food that local natives (a few of whom they had just seen for the first time) had clearly hidden from them, and stole from it:

> they found where lately a house had been, where some planks and a great kettle was remaining, and heaps of sand newly padded with their hands. Which, they digging up, found in them diverse fair Indian baskets filled with corn, . . . which seemed to them a very goodly sight. . . . So, their time limited them being expired, they returned to the ship lest they should be in fear of their safety; and took with them part of the corn.

Bradford uses a biblical analogy for this moment, comparing the Pilgrims to Jews in Exodus who "carried with them the fruits of the land and showed their brethren." Yet these fruits were from the natives, not simply the land, and in making them their own the Pilgrims displayed a similar attitude to that of Columbus taking immediate possession of the islands upon arrival.

Having established their relationship with the local indigenous community on these terms, the Pilgrims should not have been surprised that their first encounter with Native Americans was likewise a hostile one. A group of native warriors attacked the encamped Pilgrims; as Bradford writes, "The cry of the Indians was dreadful, especially when they saw the men run out of the rendezvous toward the shallop [small boat] to recover their arms, the Indians wheeling about them." It is entirely understandable that the English fought back, but when their superior firepower had chased the attackers away, they defined the experience in overarching and overtly exclusionary terms. As Bradford puts it, "Thus it pleased God to vanquish their enemies and give them deliverance." Responding to an attack with violence was likely necessary, but defining the natives as "their enemies" was not; not in this confused initial moment and not in an overarching perspective. And when Bradford adds that they "called that place the First Encounter," we can see how foundational this hostile and exclusionary moment was for the Pilgrims and their perspective on indigenous peoples.

Yet less than a year after these two divisive and hostile events, the Pilgrims and Wampanoags were sharing corn at the harvest celebration, with the only violence directed at the five deer which Massasoit and his warriors brought to the festivities. The shift was due largely to Tisquantum, and the six-point peace treaty that he—along with Samoset, a visiting Abenaki tribal leader who had learned English from fishermen near the Gulf of Maine and who served as another mediator between the communities—helped broker between Massasoit's Pokanoket Wampanoag and the Plymouth Pilgrims. The treaty was practical and political for both sides: the Pilgrims of course needed allies in this new world, and the Pokanoket, themselves decimated by illnesses in recent years, sought protection from the neighboring and potentially hostile Narragansett tribe. Yet nonetheless, this agreement, like the harvest celebration that symbolically cemented it and the cross-cultural mediators who negotiated it, illustrated the genuine possibility of an inclusive New England and American community.

Tisquantum's efforts toward that community, like those of las Casas and de Vaca in the prior century, were met with frequent resistance and suspicion, and tragically did not foreshadow the region's and hemisphere's dominant, exclusionary story of exploration and colonization, genocide and enslavement. Tisquantum himself was accused by some of the Pilgrims of fomenting violence, was nearly executed by Massasoit as a spy for the English, and died of "Indian fever" (likely another European disease) only a year after the harvest celebration. The English did maintain their peace with the Wampanaog during Massasoit's lifetime, but also fought the brutal Pequot War against other New England indigenous peoples only fifteen years after the treaty, enslaved both Native and African Americans throughout the seventeenth century, expelled more inclusive thinkers like Roger Williams (who wrote the first English guide to Native American languages), and generally enacted a more exclusionary than inclusive vision of their new American community.

So the story of the European exploration and colonization era, and especially of indigenous cultures in that period, belongs more to Columbus than to las Casas, de Vaca, and Tisquantum. It's certainly vital to remember that our shared history begins with such foundational exclusions, and to consider their legacy for twenty-first-century Native Americans and for us all. Yet it's just as crucial to highlight the inclusive visions offered by these alternative figures, the possibility of a shared, multicultural community for which they worked and argued. Postcontact America began in many ways with a battle between those exclusionary and inclusive definitions—and as that battle has raged ever since, those of us fighting for the inclusive vision must highlight and take continued inspiration from foundational figures like Bartolomé de las Casas, Álvar Nuñez Cabeza de Vaca, and Tisquantum.

Chapter Two

Slaves, Revolutionary Enemies or Exemplars

The "self-evident truths" and "inalienable rights" which opened the Declaration of Independence and drove the American Revolution—"all men are created equal"; "life, liberty, and the pursuit of happiness"—seemed strikingly and purposefully to exclude one prominent American community: African American slaves. Historians estimate that there were more than 450,000 such slaves across the 13 colonies when the Revolution began, just under 20 percent of the total population. Thomas Jefferson, who drafted the Declaration of Independence, was a slave owner, as were the author of the Constitution's Bill of Rights (George Mason) and five of the first seven presidents (including the Revolutionary War general and "Father of Our Country" George Washington). The United States Constitution even codified slavery's dehumanization of its subjects into foundational national law, defining those nearly half a million African American slaves as less than a full person (three-fifths of one, to be exact) for purposes of congressional and Electoral College representation.

A cut paragraph from Jefferson's June 28, 1776, draft of the Declaration reveals that this exclusion of African American slaves from Revolutionary definitions of America went even further, however. In this telling paragraph, Jefferson turns slavery into one of the colonists' many complaints against the English king George III, arguing that it is "he" who has "waged cruel war against human nature itself, violating its most sacred rights of life and liberty in the persons of a distant people who never offended him." Just as the Declaration as a whole represented the colonies' attempt to separate from England, this paragraph seeks to define slavery (and thus implicitly African American slaves, that "distant people") as separate from an independent

America, an external imposition on rather than an intrinsic part of this evolving new nation.

Jefferson's cut paragraph takes that exclusionary argument one step further still, playing into contemporary fears that England was encouraging slave rebellions in the colonies. He writes, "And he [King George] is now exciting those very people to rise in arms among us, and to purchase that liberty of which *he* had deprived them, by murdering the people upon whom *he* also obtruded them: thus paying off former crimes committed against the *liberties* of one people, with crimes which he urges them to commit against the *lives* of another" (Jefferson's emphases). That complex sentence extends the linkage of slavery to England with its repeated emphasis on what *he* has done, making the American slave system solely a creation of the king (and the European nation he represents). And it also further develops the concurrent argument that African American slaves were an external people who had been "obtruded" (defined as "forced in an unwelcome way") upon the American colonists.

By claiming as well that the king was "exciting those very people to rise in arms against us," Jefferson did more than amplify that sense that "they" were separate and excluded from the evolving American "us." He also positioned African American slaves as directly opposed to—indeed, as armed enemies of—the Revolutionary efforts. Even more troubling, he defined the slaves' desire to "purchase [their] liberty"—a desire that would seem quite parallel to, if not in fact precisely the same as, the quest for the "inalienable rights" of "life, liberty, and the pursuit of happiness" with which the Declaration opens—as the driving force behind their armed opposition to the Revolution. In Jefferson's vision of slavery here, both the slave system itself and the slaves' efforts to escape it seem entirely excluded from and hostile to the incipient American Revolution.

Jefferson's fears of armed slave uprisings were, it's important to note, not without historical precedent. In November 1775, John Murray, the Earl of Dunmore and the last Royal Governor of Virginia, issued a proclamation calling upon Virginia slaves to leave their owners and join the English forces. The proclamation's exact effects remain unclear, but it was logical enough that a Virginia slave owner like Jefferson would have it on his mind less than a year later. Yet by including these accusations in his draft of the Declaration, Jefferson made the issue of slavery one of the colonists' chief complaints against the king and principal arguments for independence. And by folding the specific historical subject of Dunmore's proclamation into a broader description of both slavery and prospective emancipation as imposed by England and opposed to the Revolutionary efforts, Jefferson created an exclusionary narrative that located slaves entirely outside of the emerging United States (and would have only given Dunmore more ammunition for his arguments as a result).

The Continental Congress ended up cutting that paragraph (and with it any reference to African American slavery) from the Declaration's final draft. Perhaps the group's many slave owners momentarily recognized the hypocrisy inherent in making such claims about the slave system while arguing for their own liberty, or perhaps they simply did not want to open that particular can of worms in an already controversial document. Perhaps, as historian Sean Wilentz has argued in his book *No Property in Man: Slavery and Antislavery at the Nation's Founding* (2018), such choices reflect the interplay of pro- and antislavery forces in these framing moments. But in any case, the broader, exclusionary attitudes toward African American slaves captured in Jefferson's paragraph can be directly linked to the Constitution's Three-Fifths Compromise, one of many telling ways in which this foundational American community was dehumanized by and excluded from our originating national documents and ideas. Indeed, the Revolution's motivating, "self-evident truths" that "all men are created equal" and "endowed by their Creator with certain inalienable rights" seemed to depend precisely on such exclusions.

Yet that exclusionary definition of Revolutionary America did not go unchallenged, and in fact it was African American slaves themselves who offered the most impressive and inspiring inclusive counterpoints. From a runaway slave who became one of the Revolution's first casualties and heroic symbols to a slave poet who linked her personal history and perspective to the Revolutionary cause and ideals, these African Americans illustrated how inseparable were their community and the emerging United States. And two Massachusetts slaves and their allies went further still, using the language and ideals of the Declaration of Independence and the groundbreaking 1780 Massachusetts Constitution both to argue successfully for their personal freedom and to help move their state toward the comprehensive abolition of slavery in the process.

Crispus Attucks, an African American merchant sailor in colonial Boston, was one of five protesters shot and killed by English soldiers at the March 5, 1770, Boston Massacre. Attucks, James Caldwell, and Samuel Gray were killed immediately, while Samuel Maverick died later that night, and Patrick Carr succumbed to his wounds two weeks later. Perhaps because of his unusual name, perhaps because he was always listed alphabetically first among the five victims, and certainly because he was an African American, Attucks has generally been highlighted in the massacre's immediate aftermath and in our subsequent collective memories as the first casualty of the American Revolution and one of its earliest symbolic heroes. Yet for centuries little else was known about Attucks beyond his race and his symbolic death.

In recent years historians have learned a good deal more about Attucks, however, and while certain details of his life and identity remain somewhat ambiguous, it seems clear that he was both born into and a fugitive from slavery. His father was Prince Yonger, an African-born slave in Framingham, Massachusetts; and his mother was Nanny Peterattucks, a Native American of the neighboring Natick Wampanoag tribe (and possibly a slave herself, although that detail remains unclear). Moreover, we know for a fact that Attucks ran away from slavery in Framingham in 1750 (at around the age of twenty-seven), as his master William Brown posted three newspaper advertisements looking for his runaway slave, "A Mulatto fellow, about 27 years of age, named Crispus." Records of the next two decades of Attucks's life are spotty, but at some point he joined the demographically diverse eighteenth-century Boston community of sailors for hire, serving on a whaling crew and working as a rope maker.

In the trial of the eight English soldiers accused of killing Attucks and his fellow protesters, the defense lawyer—none other than future Founding Father and president John Adams—used such details of Attucks's identity to impugn his character and motives. Attucks, Adams argued in court, had "undertaken to be the hero of the night" through his "mad behavior," but was less representative of Revolutionary heroism and more a part of the "motley rabble of saucy boys, negroes and mulattos, Irish teagues and outlandish jack tars" that comprised both the city's community of merchant sailors and the event's protesters. While such a mob was not necessarily opposed to the Revolutionary effort in the same way Jefferson would imagine slaves to be in his Declaration draft, clearly this ragtag community did not fit the more elite or organized vision of both Revolutionary resistance and American identity for which Adams (and many others) would subsequently argue.

Seen in a different light, Attucks's status as a fugitive slave turned sailor for hire marks him as a perfect embodiment of the Revolution's first activisms. Nineteenth-century Boston poet John Boyle O'Reilly would in his famous poem, "Crispus Attucks," describe Attucks as "the first to defy, the first to die," and we now know that that defiance had begun two decades before his fateful final moments on the Boston waterfront. To run away from slavery was, after all, to risk one's life in opposition to society's most powerful forces of law, government, and economics, to face insurmountable odds and obstacles in search of liberty from oppression. Yet by 1770, Attucks had succeeded in running away and making an independent life for himself among this multicultural, inclusive Boston and New England community, an unlikely personal victory that could be paralleled to the nation's eventual, communal triumph in the Revolution his protest and death helped inaugurate.

As that Revolution's opening act unfolded over the decade after the Boston Massacre, one of its most ardent literary advocates was none other than another African American slave from Massachusetts, Phillis Wheatley. Born in West Africa in the early 1750s, Wheatley had been kidnapped into slavery when she was only seven or eight years old and brought to America on an English slave ship named *The Phillis*. In July 1761, the Boston merchant John Wheatley purchased her as a maid and companion for his wife, Susanna, naming the young girl Phillis after that vessel. Susanna and the Wheatley's teenage children, Mary and Nathaniel, tutored the exceptionally bright and talented Phillis in reading, writing, religion, and classical literature, and she wrote her first poem, "To the University of Cambridge, in New England," when she was just fourteen years old.

In that poem, as in many of those collected in her 1773 first book, *Poems on Various Subjects, Religious and Moral* (which she published in England while traveling there with Nathaniel Wheatley), Wheatley weds classical, mythological, and literary allusions to Christian themes in a relatively universal or ahistorical frame. Contemporary readers of poems such as "To the University of Cambridge" would not necessarily have known that the author was an American nor that she was an African American slave. An interesting and important exception in that debut collection was Wheatley's most frequently anthologized poem, the short and complex "On Being Brought from Africa to America," which describes her spiritual conversion to Christianity in somewhat exclusionary terms (distinguishing it from the "pagan" land of her birth), yet links that personal transformation to a historically grounded, socially progressive, and inclusive argument that all "negroes" have the same potential for salvation as do any other Christians.

When Wheatley returned from England to Massachusetts in the fall of 1773, her personal transformations and progress continued, as she was emancipated by the Wheatley family and began her independent American life. At the same time, she found Massachusetts and America likewise evolving, developing independent ideals, and moving ever closer to Revolutionary conflict with England: for example, the Boston Tea Party took place on December 16, 1773, not long after Wheatley's return to the city. Over the next few years she would turn her poetic attention to that progressive historical cause, with striking results in two distinct and equally important threads that together illustrate just how fully Wheatley connected her personal perspective and identity to the Revolutionary cause.

One of those Revolutionary poetic threads is represented by "To His Excellency General Washington" (1775), one of America's earliest and most impassioned literary arguments for the Revolution. The poem builds on Wheatley's prior classical and mythological themes, imploring the Muses and the goddess Freedom to bless her titular subject and the cause he is leading. She likewise weds that Revolutionary cause to her spiritual perspective on America as a chosen land, warning "whoever dares disgrace/The land of freedom's heaven-defended race" that they will encounter "Columbia's fury." Yet she also makes the Revolutionary case in more overtly contemporary and political terms, noting that "fix'd are the eyes of nations on the scales,/For in their hopes Columbia's arm prevails," and imploring General Washington to "Proceed, great chief, with virtue on thy side."

Wheatley's poetic support for and connection to Washington and the Revolution did not simply stay on the page. In late October 1775, she sent a copy of the poem to Washington himself at his headquarters in nearby Cambridge, Massachusetts, accompanying it with a brief letter of explanation for the recent historical events that had "excite[d] sensations not easy to suppress" and led her to take such a bold step. Washington responded in February 1776 with a letter of his own, expressing his appreciation for both the poem and the poet, since its "style and manner exhibit a striking proof of your great Poetical talents." He concluded with a striking invitation: "should you ever come to Cambridge, . . . I shall be happy to see a person so favored by the Muses, and to whom nature has been so liberal and beneficent in her dispensations." Wheatley may have taken him up on his offer and visited headquarters in March 1776; the historical records of that potential meeting are scarce and uncertain, but its enduring legend itself reflects the connection of Wheatley to Washington and the unfolding Revolution.

Whether she met with Washington in March or not, Wheatley's poetic tribute to the general would gain even more widespread attention a month later, as it was published by none other than Revolutionary pamphleteer Thomas Paine in the April 2, 1776, issue of the *Pennsylvania Magazine* (which he was editing at the time). Washington had shared Wheatley's poem with his friend and Continental Army comrade Joseph Reed in February, and Reed had passed it along to the fellow Philadelphian Paine. Paine's fiery and best-selling proindependence pamphlet, *Common Sense*, published anonymously on January 10, 1776, and first linked to Paine on March 30 (just three days before he published Wheatley's poem), has long been described as the most overt literary argument for the Revolutionary cause. But Paine's decision to publish Wheatley's poem in his magazine at the height of the pre-Declaration fervor—Jefferson and the Continental Congress would begin drafting the Declaration two months later—makes clear just how much he saw "To His Excellency George Washington" as a complementary Revolutionary text.

Although Wheatley had become famous as a slave poet with the publication of her 1773 collection, there's nothing in "To His Excellency George Washington" that is in any specific way linked to—and certainly no idea or sentiment there that necessarily depends on—her experiences of slavery. Neither did she overtly define herself as a former slave nor an African American in her accompanying letter to Washington. But Wheatley's other most overtly Revolutionary poem, "To the Right Honourable William, Earl of Dartmouth" (1774), does make explicit and central the connection between slavery and Revolution in her identity and perspective, and thus represents a second and even more inclusive thread in her poetic engagements with that evolving national community.

William Legge, the Earl of Dartmouth, was at the time the newly appointed English secretary of state for the colonies (a role in which he served from 1772 to 1775), and a man whose position on the tense and evolving relationship between the colonies and England was famously considered undecided. Wheatley, encouraged by the English merchant Thomas Woolridge, a supporter of Legge's and of the colonies whom she had met while in London the previous year, addressed her poem to this important figure directly in order to make the case for American freedom and independence.

As in the Washington poem, for most of "Earl of Dartmouth" Wheatley uses mythological and spiritual allusions to make that case, linking "New-England" to "the Goddess . . . Fair Freedom," and expressing her earnest hope that under Legge's care "Freedom's charms [will] unfold" once more. If Legge follows that course, she boldly asserts, it will likewise result in his personal salvation; she ends the poem with an image of her addressee carried "upwards to that blest abode,/Where, like the prophet, thou shalt find thy God." If Wheatley's poem and letter to Washington reflect a striking level of self-assurance and self-confidence in her role as a poetic messenger of such Revolutionary sentiments, "Earl of Dartmouth" goes even further, with the poet ultimately positioning herself as a purveyor of—and her American home as a concurrent receptacle for—nothing less than divine truths.

Yet that's not the most striking aspect of Wheatley's perspective in this Revolutionary poem. In the second stanza (of four), she portrays America as a slave to England: "No longer shalt dread the iron chain,/Which wanton Tyranny with lawless hand/Had made, and with it meant t'enslave the land." Up to that point in the poem, a reader might not know of Wheatley's own status as a former slave; or, perhaps, as a slave still, since she had not yet been emancipated when Woolridge first encouraged her to write to Legge. But the next and most important stanza makes that fact and its crucial connection to the poem's Revolutionary arguments clear, and is worth quoting in full:

> Should you, my lord, while you peruse my song,
> Wonder from whence my love of Freedom sprung,
> Whence flow these wishes for the common good,
> By feeling hearts alone best understood,
> I, young in life, by seeming cruel fate
> Was snatch'd from Afric's fancy'd happy seat:
> What pangs excruciating must molest,
> What sorrows labour in my parent's breast?
> Steel'd was that soul and by no misery mov'd
> That from a father seiz'd his babe belov'd:
> Such, such my case. And can I then but pray

Others may never feel tyrannic sway?

"Such, such my case." It's difficult to imagine a more direct and convincing alternative to Jefferson's assertion that slaves' desire for liberty represents a foreign and opposing force to the American Revolutionary efforts. As Wheatley argues so persuasively in these powerful lines, there could be no American community more aware of what tyranny and freedom mean, respectively, than African American slaves. And thus there could be no community more committed to "the common good" of liberty and equality than those who had felt the "tyrannic sway," the iron chain, of slavery. What the fugitive slave Crispus Attucks demonstrated through his actions at the Boston Massacre, the Boston slave and freedwoman Phillis Wheatley makes clear in literary moments like this: that the American Revolution not only included African American slaves, it took on a special significance for them.

That significance was only amplified once the Revolution commenced in earnest, and its founding ideals began to be put into practice by the newly formed United States. Perhaps not coincidentally, it was once again in Massachusetts where the link between African American slaves and the Revolution's ideas and ideals became clearest. Massachusetts was the first of the newly created states to approve a constitution, with the Constitutional Convention (apparently the first such event in world history) beginning on September 1, 1779, and the final document approved by voters on June 15, 1780. And shortly thereafter, two African American slaves and their legal and abolitionist allies used the language of the Declaration of Independence and the laws embodied in that 1780 Massachusetts Constitution to argue successfully for their personal freedom and rights, changing the history of slavery in their state and modeling an inclusive Revolutionary American community in the process.

When that groundbreaking Massachusetts Constitutional Convention met to draft the state's Constitution, its participants chose to begin the document with as clear an echo of the Declaration of Independence as possible. The first section was entitled "A Declaration of the Rights of the Inhabitants of the Commonwealth of Massachusetts," and the opening Article I read in full, "All men are born free and equal, and have certain natural, essential, and unalienable rights; among which may be reckoned the right of enjoying and defending their lives and liberties; that of acquiring, possessing, and protecting property; in fine, that of seeking and obtaining their safety and happiness." Moreover, while the Declaration of Independence was simply a statement of principles, the Massachusetts Constitution represented a legal framework for governance and society. As a result, this opening turned the Declaration's ideals of freedom and equality into legal rights that would form the basis for "The Frame of Government" that the Massachusetts Constitution's second section would enumerate.

Yet in 1780 Massachusetts, as in every state in the emerging United States at the time, slavery was legal. A 1754 census had listed nearly 4,500 Massachusetts slaves, more than 2 percent of the colony's total population, and the community remained steady (if it did not indeed continue to grow) over the next few decades. Our national narratives of slavery and the Revolution almost always link the system entirely to the Southern colonies: see for example the portrayals of framing debates over slavery in the popular musicals *1776* (1969) and *Hamilton* (2015), both of which pit Southern slave owners, such as Jefferson, against Northern opponents. In reality, however, slavery was a thoroughly national system at the time of the Declaration and Revolution, and the statement of "natural, essential, and unalienable rights" that opened the 1780 Massachusetts Constitution thus seemed as necessarily exclusionary of African American slaves as had been the Declaration's ideals.

Massachusetts slaves and their abolitionist allies did not accept that exclusionary vision of freedom and rights in the state, however. As early as January 13, 1777, a group of slaves (aided by such abolitionist allies) filed a petition to the state legislature, describing themselves as "a great number of blacks detained in a state of slavery in the bowels of a free and Christian country," and echoing the language of the Declaration of Independence to make the case for "a natural and unalienable right to that freedom which the Great Parent of the Universe hath bestowed equally on all mankind and which they have never forfeited by any compact or agreement whatever." The petition did not result in any state laws or collective moves toward abolition; but when the 1780 Constitution opened with its own invocation of such natural and unalienable rights, two Massachusetts slaves were ready to make their own successful and influential cases for inclusive visions of freedom and equality.

Elizabeth ("Bett" or "Mumbet") Freeman was a well-known herbalist and midwife in the western Massachusetts town of Sheffield, where she was a slave of the Ashley family. She had been born a slave in Claverack, New York, in the early 1740s, but in the 1750s she was brought to Sheffield when her master's daughter, Hannah Hogeboom, married Colonel John Ashley (a veteran of the French and Indian War). Ashley would become a noted business and political leader in the town, and it was in his home that eleven prominent community members signed the January 12, 1773, Sheffield Resolves (also known as the Sheffield Declaration, and printed publicly in the local paper *The Massachusetts Spy, or, Thomas's Boston Journal* on February 18). That influential document, long seen as a direct predecessor to the Declaration of Independence, opened with a resolution that "mankind in a state of nature are equal, free, and independent of each other, and have a right to the undisturbed enjoyment of their lives, their liberty and property."

Freeman, who like many slaves never learned to read or write (teaching slaves to do so was not illegal in eighteenth-century Massachusetts, but it was still far from standard practice), quite possibly did not know of the Sheffield Resolves. But in 1780, she heard the newly approved Massachusetts Constitution read aloud at a public gathering in Sheffield, and was immediately struck by its opening assertion of shared rights. The next day, she approached Theodore Sedgwick, a young Sheffield lawyer, well-known abolitionist, and one of the eleven signees of the Sheffield Resolves. According to the account provided by Sedgwick's daughter Catharine Maria Sedgwick, later one of the early nineteenth century's most successful American novelists, Freeman argued to Theodore, "I heard that paper read yesterday, that says, all men are created equal, and that every man has a right to freedom. I'm not a dumb critter; won't the law give me my freedom?"

Theodore Sedgwick agreed to take Freeman's case, pairing it with that of Brom, another slave in the Ashley household and likely one brought into the cause by Freeman herself. Recognizing the case's significance, both for the abolitionist cause and for the question of what the new Massachusetts Constitution would mean for law and justice in the state, Sedgwick partnered with Tapping Reeve, one of the region's most prominent young lawyers (and subsequent founder of the Litchfield [Connecticut] Law School, one of the nation's first such institutions). Together, the two lawyers brought *Brom and Bett v. Ashley* before the County Court of Common Pleas in Great Barrington in May 1781, arguing there that the Constitution's Article I rendered slavery in Massachusetts illegal.

The jury ruled in Freeman and Brom's favor, finding that "Brom & Bett are not, nor were they at the time of the purchase of the original writ the legal Negro[es] of the said John Ashley." Defining them legally as workers rather than slaves, the court awarded financial compensation for their labor as well as punitive damages; per the court transcript, Ashley immediately asserted his intention to appeal the verdict, but subsequently decided to drop his appeal and accept the decision as "final and binding." Indeed, he would later ask Freeman to return to his household as a paid servant, but she declined, choosing instead to work as a domestic servant and governess in the Sedgwick household. It was there where Catharine Maria Sedgwick (the second youngest of the family's ten children) would come to know her as Mumbet, an important figure and relationship about which Catharine would write at length in her 1853 piece "Slavery in New England" (published in *Bentley's Miscellany*).

Despite the clear precedent set by this verdict, Freeman's case might not have been as immediately and profoundly influential were it not for a strikingly similar, if even more complicated and crucial, case making its way through the Massachusetts courts at precisely the same time. Its subject, Quock (sometimes spelled Quok) Walker, had been born into slavery in Massachusetts in 1753, and shortly after his birth his entire family was bought by James Caldwell of Worcester County. Caldwell apparently promised Walker his freedom when Walker reached the age of twenty-five, but after Caldwell's death his widow remarried Nathaniel Jennison, and Walker's new master did not hold to the promise. In 1781, at the age of twenty-eight, Walker ran away from the Jennison farm, going to work at a nearby farm for two of his former master's brothers (John and Seth Caldwell). Jennison found him there and returned him to a state of slavery, beating him brutally in the process. Jennison and Walker then filed separate civil lawsuits: Jennison suing the Caldwells for stealing his property and Walker suing Jennison for battery. The two cases were heard concurrently by the Worcester County Court of Common Pleas in June 1781.

Initially, the court rendered split verdicts on these two questions: finding in Jennison's favor against the Caldwells and awarding him twenty-five pounds in damages; and yet likewise finding that Walker was a free man under the 1780 Constitution and awarding him fifty pounds in damages for his illegal beating. The contrasting decisions reflected slavery's ambiguous status in 1781 Massachusetts. Slavery was still legal on its own terms, and thus a slave like Quock Walker was still the legal property of his master and could not go to work for anyone else. And yet the system existed in direct opposition to the framing principles of the state's new Constitution, under which every inhabitant of Massachusetts was entitled to the rights and freedoms for which Freeman's and Walker's cases argued. To help resolve this contradictory tension, the two verdicts were both appealed to the Massachusetts Supreme Judicial Court, which heard the cases in September 1781.

The Supreme Judicial Court's decisions both went in Walker's favor: throwing out Jennison's appeal of the battery verdict and overturning the theft verdict, finding that Walker was a free man and thus could be legally employed by the Caldwells. The court and the state took the opportunity to go one significant step further: the Massachusetts attorney general filed his own case against Jennison, *Commonwealth v. Jennison*, citing the Freeman decision as well as the Supreme Judicial Court verdicts on Walker's behalf to argue that slavery in Massachusetts was unconstitutional and illegal. In rendering a 1783 decision in favor of the commonwealth's position, Supreme Judicial Court Chief Justice William Cushing wrote a genuinely stunning paragraph that crystallized the relationship between the Massachusetts Constitution, the American Revolution, and the abolition of slavery, and that is worth quoting in full:

> As to the doctrine of slavery and the right of Christians to hold Africans in perpetual servitude, and sell and treat them as we do our horses and cattle, that

has been heretofore countenanced by the Province Laws formerly, but no-
where is it expressly enacted or established. It has been a usage—a usage
which took its origin from the practice of some of the European nations, and
the regulations of British government respecting the then Colonies, for the
benefit of trade and wealth. But whatever sentiments have formerly prevailed
in this particular or slid in upon us by the example of others, a different idea
has taken place with the people of America, more favorable to the natural
rights of mankind, and to that natural, innate desire of Liberty, with which
Heaven (without regard to color, complexion, or shape of noses-features) has
inspired all the human race. And upon this ground our Constitution of Government, by which the people of this Commonwealth have solemnly bound themselves, sets out with declaring that all men are born free and equal—and that
every subject is entitled to liberty, and to have it guarded by the laws, as well
as life and property—and in short is totally repugnant to the idea of being born
slaves. This being the case, I think the idea of slavery is inconsistent with our
own conduct and Constitution; and there can be no such thing as perpetual
servitude of a rational creature, unless his liberty is forfeited by some criminal
conduct or given up by personal consent or contract.

I'm not sure a more inclusive legal opinion or document can be found anywhere in American history. Cushing defines this foundational American "different idea" as precisely an all-encompassing desire for liberty, an ideal that
extends to and "has inspired all the human race." The Declaration's and
Massachusetts Constitution's use of the phrase "all men" may not have had
purposefully gendered connotations (it was the period's general usage), but
with "all the human race" Cushing nevertheless goes an important step further. This is an argument that American laws and ideals apply equally and
fully to every person with no distinctions or hierarchies, a truly inclusive
definition of our national foundations and community.

   That 1783 Supreme Judicial Court decision, coupled with the earlier
Walker verdicts and the Freeman case, led directly to the comprehensive
abolition of slavery in Massachusetts. Interestingly, that abolition was entirely voluntary—that is, no law was passed, nor was the state constitution
amended in any way. Instead, slave owners responded to these court decisions and subsequent communal efforts and pressures by voluntarily freeing
their slaves, such as by changing the arrangements to those of wage labor or
indentured servitude (among other steps). While this voluntary form of abolition might seem haphazard or uncertain, it produced the desired results in
less than a decade: the 1790 federal census (the first undertaken by the post-
Revolution and post-Constitution United States government) recorded no
slaves in Massachusetts. Indeed, compared to other Northern states (many of
which passed gradual abolition laws that kept some state inhabitants enslaved
for decades to come), Massachusetts's voluntary abolition—driven first and
foremost by the grassroots efforts of Freeman, Walker, and their allies—
succeeded in eradicating slavery far more quickly and thoroughly.

It would be easy to credit the 1780 Massachusetts Constitution, and particularly that opening article on natural and unalienable rights to freedom and equality, with helping produce (or at least make possible) this model of abolition. Yet it's important to reiterate that that Constitution was created in, and in its own details in no overt way opposed to, a state where slavery was legal, where many thousands of residents were by both law and social practice denied those fundamental rights from birth to death. The 1780 Constitution, that is, created a system of laws and rights that was at the time and on its own terms just as exclusionary toward African American slaves as was the Declaration of Independence's opening statement of self-evident truths. Neither the final draft of the Declaration nor the Massachusetts Constitution defined slavery and slaves as the overtly foreign and hostile presence that Jefferson's cut paragraph did; but both founding documents could easily accommodate and further an exclusionary vision of a Revolutionary America with seemingly no place for African American slaves.

Yet at the same time, each of these founding documents and moments could and did serve instead as a starting point for extending American ideals to even our most dispossessed fellow citizens. What it took were the efforts of Elizabeth Freeman, Quock Walker, and their allies to reframe the Massachusetts Constitution and its rights and freedoms in an inclusive way, just as it took the activism of fugitive slave Crispus Attucks and the poetry of former slave Phillis Wheatley to reframe the American Revolution as a complement to African Americans' quests for liberty, independence, and equality. These disparate and unique yet parallel and interconnected African American figures and voices offered an alternative vision of the Revolution and of the American ideals and identity it would help inaugurate. Their lives, writings, and triumphs make clear that slaves and African Americans were neither the obtruded distant people nor the armed enemies of Jefferson's exclusionary fears; they were a vital part of an inclusive new national identity and community.

Chapter Three

Indian Removal and Inspiring Resistance

President Andrew Jackson's policy of Indian Removal, and more exactly the horrific and tragic Trail of Tears that it produced, is among the exclusionary histories most familiar to twenty-first-century Americans. This signature Jackson administration policy, pursued immediately, consistently, and in direct opposition to a Supreme Court ruling, forcibly uprooted tens of thousands of Native Americans from a handful of Southeastern American tribes, setting them on a cross-country winter death march toward distant "Indian Territory" that killed thousands and permanently affected all who experienced it. The striking scope, cruelty, and inhumanity of the Trail of Tears makes it stand out across the centuries of destructive moments and policies engendered by exclusionary definitions of America, and at least in its broad stokes it is widely and effectively remembered.

Yet as brutal and ugly as the Trail of Tears was, and as important as it is to continue remembering it, it was the federal Indian Removal policy itself that most overtly represented a shift in perspective toward a more exclusionary national definition. As I detailed in chapter 1, European explorers and settlers had taken such exclusionary attitudes toward indigenous peoples and the evolving American community since the first moments of contact. Yet for the first half-century after the American Revolution and the political founding of the United States, the new U.S. federal government had generally dealt with Native American tribes in a somewhat more nuanced and thoughtful manner. Those federal policies were based on treating each tribe as a distinct and unique community, and on then engaging with the particular issues facing those numerous American communities and their relationship to the new and expanding United States.

That respectful and relatively inclusive attitude extended to early laws that affected Native Americans more broadly, such as the Northwest Ordinance of 1787. That first post-Revolutionary legal addition of new territory to the United States included this sentence:

> The utmost good faith shall always be observed towards the Indians; their lands and property shall never be taken from them without their consent; and, in their property, rights, and liberty, they shall never be invaded or disturbed, unless in just and lawful wars authorized by Congress; but laws founded in justice and humanity, shall from time to time be made for preventing wrongs being done to them, and for preserving peace and friendship with them.

While of course European American settlers could and did violate this sentiment in practice, the law's language still reflected an inclusive federal attitude and policy toward Native Americans.

All of that changed, immediately and drastically, after Andrew Jackson's March 4, 1829, presidential inauguration. The changes were likely not a surprise to many Americans, since one of Jackson's chief claims to fame was as an "Indian killer," the commanding general in a number of particularly bloody and brutal wars against Southeastern Native American tribes. The Cherokee themselves had given him that hostile nickname; the Creek knew him as "Sharp Knife" for similar reasons. Such early nineteenth-century wars were far bigger than any one commander, of course. Yet as the Northwest Ordinance noted, conduct during "just and lawful wars" between the federal government and Native American tribes was one thing, and peaceful dealings and relationships between these respective groups outside of those wartime moments quite another. The policies enacted by the Jackson administration treated Native Americans by default and continually in precisely the exclusionary and hostile ways illustrated by his "Indian killer" past and reputation.

In his first State of the Union address as president (then known as the President's Annual Message to Congress and delivered on December 8, 1829), Jackson explicitly called for the removal of all native tribes beyond the borders of the United States. He couched that call in ostensible fears for their future, stating that "this fate [disappearance] surely awaits them if they remain within the limits of the States." Jackson would reiterate this seeming concern for Native American survival multiple times over the next few years, but many of the arguments that he relied on most consistently in order to justify this supposed fear were telling and directly paralleled key elements of the federal Indian Removal policies his administration would enact.

For one thing, Jackson time and again collapsed all Native Americans into a single entity, eliding distinctions between the tribes and defining them all as both outside of the United States and distinctly inferior to that nation's citizens. This was never clearer than in his fifth message to Congress, on December 3, 1833, when he argued,

That those tribes cannot exist surrounded by our settlements and in continual contact with our citizens is certain. They have neither the intelligence, the industry, the moral habits, nor the desire of improvement which are essential to any favorable change in their condition. Established in the midst of another and a superior race, and without appreciating the causes of their inferiority or seeking to control them, they must necessarily yield to the force of circumstances and ere long disappear.

Jackson's first shift in federal policy reflected this white supremacist attitude precisely. While prior administrations had dealt with individual tribes specifically, seeking to engage with the particular circumstances and issues in each case, the Jackson administration from the outset defined all Native Americans as one community. Only by collapsing those individual distinctions could Jackson then define Native Americans as a collective "inferior race," one located physically "in the midst of" yet in this discriminatory vision separate from and opposed to the "superior race" of Americans. This attitude and policy of sweeping separation and definition was a vital prerequisite to any arguments for removing Native Americans from the United States.

Jackson's arguments for Indian Removal also depended on a consistent vision of the states as more important, and more in need of federal protection, than these indigenous peoples within their borders. In that December 1829 address, he framed states' rights as precisely such a corollary to his removal plans: "A State cannot be dismembered by Congress or restricted in the exercise of her constitutional power." Yet since Native Americans were residents of all the states, what Jackson truly meant was that both the state governments and his federal government would privilege and protect the interests and needs of European Americans within those states. Indeed, the conflicts that had precipitated this change in federal policy consistently pitted white settlers and state governments against native tribes, such as the case of the white settlers in Georgia who (with the full support of the state government) sought to take lands belonging to the Cherokee in which there was believed to be gold and other resources. The newly formed Jackson administration promised Georgia that it would "extinguish Indian title" within the state as soon as possible, another key factor in the move toward a federal removal policy.

In May 1830, five months after Jackson's 1829 address and following a period of intense debate, Congress turned that policy and those exclusionary attitudes into federal law, passing the Indian Removal Act. The law overtly gave the president and federal government the power to "extinguish the Indian claim" to any lands in their possession, disingenuously calling this process an "exchange of lands with the Indians residing in any of the states or territories." It's difficult to overstate how fully this law conflicted with the Constitution and Bill of Rights and their guarantees of individual and communal protection—of property just as much as life and liberty—from an overreaching federal government. By its very existence, then, the Removal Act supported and extended Jackson's position that Native Americans were a race inferior to and outside of European American communities, one for whom the fundamental rights and liberties promised to all other Americans had no meaning.

Much of what followed the Removal Act is present in our collective memories: Jackson's use of the army to forcibly remove native tribes and send them on the Trail of Tears; the attempt by Chief Justice John Marshall's Supreme Court to challenge the constitutionality of the Removal Act with its decision in *Worcester v. Georgia* (1832); and Jackson's refusal to abide by that Supreme Court ruling, one more reflection of how committed he was to enacting and executing the removal policy (law, Constitution, and American ideals be damned). Yet all those policies and histories extended directly from the exclusionary attitude toward and definition of Native Americans that Jackson brought with him to the presidency and made a fundamental and enduring feature of our federal government. It was that attitude and definition which made possible the reservation system, reform schools designed to "kill the Indian and save the man," the denial of American citizenship to Native Americans until the 1920s, and many more destructive national policies.

In all those ways, Andrew Jackson helped shift the federal government and the United States toward a more exclusionary and white supremacist definition and treatment of Native Americans. Yet by focusing our collective memories of the era on the Trail of Tears, we have overemphasized those exclusionary histories and largely forgotten a number of striking Native American voices and activisms that resisted removal and reflected instead a more inclusive vision of America. The Cherokee themselves produced a series of communally authored and signed memorials that embodied an inspiring, inclusive alternative to the Removal Act. In Massachusetts over the same years, the Mashpee tribe succeeded at using both their own voices and the state's political system to argue for their rights and land. William Apess, the Native American minister and orator who spearheaded the Mashpee activism, wrote a pair of stunning pieces that exemplified the new definitions of American identity, history, and community that can result when native voices and stories are included in them.

By highlighting the Cherokee here, I don't mean to repeat in any way the tendency to focus on them too singly in our collective memories and narratives of the Removal era and the Trail of Tears. The Indian Removal Act was purposefully written broadly and generally in order to affect all Native American tribes, and in its first decade alone was used as the legal justification to remove a handful of Southeastern tribes, including not only the Cherokee but also the Chickasaw, Choctaw, Creek/Muscogee, and Seminoles. It was likewise applied in the same period to a number of tribes elsewhere in the expanding nation, including many in the Northwest Territory (such as the Kickapoo, Lenape/Delaware, Meskwaki/Fox, Ottawa, Potawatomi, Sauk, and Shawnee) and various branches of the Seneca in New York. By the end of the nineteenth century, the nationwide system of removal and reservations meant that this discriminatory and exclusionary federal policy had been applied to virtually every Native American tribe.

One reason for the consistent focus on the Cherokee in our histories of Indian Removal has been that key aspects of the tribe's identity directly undermine Andrew Jackson's white supremacist rhetoric of an "inferior race." By 1830, the tribe had developed a very well-established agricultural and economic system, a written language and printing press that, beginning in February 1828, were used to publish the tribal newspaper, the *Cherokee Phoenix*, and other features that made the Cherokee one of the early nineteenth century's most self-sufficient and sophisticated American communities. To be clear, the removal policy was just as discriminatory and exclusionary toward every Native American tribe and community, regardless of specifics or circumstances, but these unique and impressive details of the Cherokee community certainly reflect how inaccurate and racist it was to define native tribes as comprising a single, "inferior race," as did the Jackson administration's exclusionary, white supremacist rhetoric and policies.

The Cherokee's specific circumstances and identity also allowed them to produce a unique and crucial series of late 1820s and early 1830s documents. These written petitions and protests against the federal removal policy and law, known collectively as Memorials of the Cherokee Nation, were likely drafted by two of the tribe's principal chiefs, John Ross and John Rollin Ridge, perhaps with the aid of Elias Boudinot, the editor of the *Cherokee Phoenix* (in which they were reprinted). But they were authored in the first-person plural "we" of "the Cherokee Nation," signed by thousands of members of the tribe, and represented a communal and impressive voice, perspective, and inclusive alternative in response to the Jackson administration's exclusionary rhetoric, policies, and law.

"Inclusive" might seem like an odd word to use in this context, since the phrase "Cherokee Nation" reflects a central thread of the memorials: an emphasis on the tribe's sovereign national identity, one separate from and equal to that of the United States. This concept of Native American sovereignty, which had been a part of indigenous responses to European American settlers and governments since the first moments of contact and remains an important political and legal idea and conversation into the twenty-first century, is far too multilayered and complex for me to do justice to it here. My use of "inclusive" is in no way an attempt to ignore that question of sovereignty or reduce a tribe like the Cherokee to the status of "wards of the state," a phrase used by the Supreme Court to describe the tribe in their initial, pro–Removal Act decision in *Cherokee Nation v. Georgia* (1831).

However, sovereignty only becomes a form of exclusion of Native Americans from definitions of American identity—a more self-determining form of exclusion than white supremacy or forced removal, but an exclusionary idea nonetheless—if we equate "American identity" with our federal government or political status as a nation. Throughout this book, my vision of an inclusive American community is far broader and deeper than any such emphasis on government or politics. Here, an inclusive definition of America means an understanding of all American cultures and communities as part of our collective identity. In that light, the sovereignty question is answered: Native American communities such as the Cherokee have been and remain a vital part of such an inclusive national definition.

The Cherokee Memorials themselves offer a number of images of and arguments for such inclusion. On a broad level, both their overarching purpose and the structures of address that come with it place the Cherokee in direct and meaningful conversation with an evolving American community in the early nineteenth century. The memorials were delivered directly to the United States Congress, and each begins with an address to "the Honorable Senate and House of Representatives of the United States of America, in Congress assembled." Yet at the same time, beginning with the December 18, 1829, memorial (drafted not long after Jackson's first Address to Congress) and continuing throughout the remainder of the series, the memorials address that congressional audience as "Brothers." "We address you according to usage adopted by our forefathers," that memorial notes, but the choice is more than simply one of tradition. It indicates a relationship that is neither as hierarchical and patronizing as "wards of the state" nor as distant and disconnected as separate nations, but rather a familial bond based on equality and mutuality, what an 1836 Cherokee Memorial would call "a common interest" between these parties. And this familial structure of address calls upon these U.S. representatives to respond as they would to any such intimate, interconnected relation.

That December 1829 memorial also includes a particularly clear and compelling argument for the Cherokee's ties to their Georgia homeland. "We love, we dearly love our country," they write, "and it is due to your honorable bodies, as well as to us, to make known why we think the country is ours." They go on to argue, "The land on which we stand, we have received as an inheritance from our fathers, who possessed it from time immemorial, as a gift from our common father in heaven. We have already said, that when the white man came to the shores of America, our ancestors were found in peaceable possession of this very land. They bequeathed it to us as their children, and we have sacredly kept it as containing the remains of our beloved men. This right of inheritance we have never ceded, nor ever forfeited. Permit us to ask, what better right can a people have to a country, than the right of inheritance and immemorial peaceable possession?" Again, if we define America not through its federal government but through a place and a history that are communally inhabited and shared, the Memorial makes clear that Native American tribes such as the Cherokee have a particularly strong claim to that collective identity.

One of the memorials' originating rhetorical strategies reflects a different kind of claim to American traditions. The memorials appeal to a number of different sources to support their arguments, including treaties, past interactions with leaders such as George Washington, religion and the Golden Rule of "do to others as ye would that others should do to you," and theories of natural law and human rights. Yet perhaps the most striking source is none other than the U.S. Constitution. The first memorial, dated November 5, 1829, begins with phrases that directly echo the opening of the Constitution's Preamble: "We, the representatives of the people of the Cherokee Nation, in general council convened." Later in that same memorial, the authors quote the Constitution's Article VI directly, arguing that this section on the "sacredness of treaties, made under the authority of the United States, is paramount and supreme, stronger than the laws and constitution of any state." And the next paragraph highlights how the Cherokee have developed their own parallel form of governance: "the adoption, on our part, of a constitutional form of government, . . . which has in no wise violated the intercourse and connection which bind us to the United States [and] its constitution."

That connection, like the Cherokee's arguments for sovereignty, is a complex and multilayered one, built gradually through each of the memorials and their distinct circumstances and arguments. But the overall effect of this series of documents could not be clearer: this is a culture that is afforded by both American history and American law a set of rights that should not be curtailed and that should instead guarantee them consideration and equality within an unfolding American present and community. In an era dominated by exclusionary rhetoric toward Native Americans, the memorials model an alternative, inclusive vision of their presence and future in America. That Jackson's exclusionary, white supremacist policies and law won out is the reason why we must remember the tragedies of removal and the Trail of Tears—but we must also and especially better remember and extend the work of the impressive and inclusive voice and perspective found in the memorials of the Cherokee Nation.

While the Cherokee's inclusive activism and documents were unfortunately not able to stop those exclusionary policies and the resulting tragic histories, in Massachusetts over the same years another Native American community did successfully protest and write its way to self-determination and full inclusion in the state's legal and civic narratives. Supported by centuries of

American history and tradition in their Cape Cod setting, and aided by a controversial, eloquent young firebrand of a Pequot orator and itinerant Methodist minister, the multitribal Mashpee (often spelled "Marshpee" in the era) community resisted both white settler intrusions and a hostile state government, winning the legislative and legal authority to maintain their American community and their rights to liberty and land within it.

The Native American community in Mashpee developed out of both the most exclusionary and the most inclusive sides to American history. As I describe in chapter 1, the Wampanoag tribe was one of the first to encounter English arrivals in New England, and over the course of the seventeenth century (despite the six-point peace treaty negotiated by Chief Massasoit with the help of Tisquantum) they suffered some of the most destructive effects of those postcontact histories. While those histories included overtly violent events such as the mid-1670s King Philip's War (in which "King Philip," the English name for Chief Metacomet, and many of his Wampanoag brethren were killed), they also and especially featured a consistent thread of English settlers taking land and resources from Wampanoag villages. The Wampanoag men and women who endured these incursions and removals, and who survived the epidemics that the European arrivals brought with them, began to gather in "Indian town," a community that sprang up in the Cape Cod area known as Mashpee.

Yet if the town was thus created in part out of tragic necessity, it also represented a self-determined and inclusive model for Native American community in this postcontact America. Native Americans from other local tribes began to move into the area as well, and in 1665, two Wampanoag chiefs formally deeded the land to this burgeoning, multicultural native community. The deed, filed in Plymouth Court, noted that Mashpee would belong to these indigenous inhabitants "forever; so not to be given, sold, or alienated from them by anyone without all their consents thereunto." The town and community continued to expand and thrive for the next century, and on June 14, 1763, the Massachusetts General Court officially incorporated Mashpee as a "plantation," the colony's designation for a civic space belonging to its local residents. Yet with this recognition came a step backwards in the community's development: the patronizing appointment of white "overseers."

Over the next half century, neighboring white settlers took advantage of that status—and of the general atmosphere of exclusionary rhetoric and attitudes that would culminate in the kinds of conflicts that precipitated the Indian Removal Act—to pilfer resources from Mashpee. Firewood was frequently stolen from the community's forests, and fish and shellfish from its Cape Cod waters. Not only did the white overseers not challenge nor stop these behaviors, but they actively encouraged them, allowing neighboring white farmers to lease grazing land for their livestock and (per the Mashpee community's frequent and unanswered pleas to the state legislature) keeping the money for themselves. Moreover, when a Native American preacher known as "Blind Joe" Amos sought to lead a congregation of those in the town who had converted to Christianity, the state's appointed white minister barred him from using the meeting house, forcing him to conduct his services outside.

The expulsion of Amos and his congregation happened in the early 1830s, perhaps inspired by—and certainly in keeping with—the exclusionary national narrative produced by the Removal Act. At the same time, however, an important new presence came to Mashpee: a passionate and eloquent itinerant Methodist minister named William Apess. Apess (on whom more below) had spent the last few years traveling throughout New England, preaching to indigenous communities, and speaking and writing about Native American history, identity, religion, and community, blending both Christian and traditional spirituality and stories (such as those of his Pequot ancestors and of King Philip, to whom he claimed relation on his mother's side) with political and legal arguments. He had heard about the issues facing Mashpee, both religious and territorial, and in early 1833 he traveled to the community to see what he could contribute on each of those levels.

Ready to challenge their intrusive neighbors and ineffective overseers, and encouraged by this activist visitor to pursue self-governance, the Mashpee elected a twelve-man council. Three of those councilmen, Israel Amos (a relative of Blind Joe's), Isaac Coombs, and Ezra Attaquin, would later write, in a letter to the state legislature in support of Apess, that "the Great Spirit who is the friend of the Indian as well as of the white man, has raised up among you a brother of our own and has sent him to us that he might show us all the secret contrivances of the pale faces to deceive and defraud us." The council and tribe had, they added, "all the confidence in him that we can put in any man," and inspired by that confidence, the council worked with Apess to draft a formal document of protest, a petition sent "to the Governor & Council of the State of Massachusetts" on May 21, 1833.

That petition, signed by 108 men and women from the community and collectively authored "on behalf of the Mashpee Tribe" and "in the voice of one man," had two overtly practical purposes: to lodge a series of protests about the abuses perpetrated by both white neighbors and state overseers; and to set a date of July 1, 1833, as a line of demarcation, after which the tribe would "not permit any white man to come upon our plantation to cut or carry off wood or hay or any other article." But along with those accounts and resolutions was a more philosophical and inclusive statement: "That we as a Tribe will rule ourselves, and have the right to do so for all men are born free and Equal, says the Constitution of the country." As with the Cherokee Memorials, this was a statement of tribal sovereignty, but one that located them firmly within the contexts of American law, history, and identity, and indeed called upon those contexts as support for the tribe's rights.

Both the neighboring and official white communities responded to this document in overtly hostile and exclusionary ways. On July 1, the very date set by the tribe as the start of formal resistance, two men from the nearby town of Barnstable arrived in Mashpee to test the tribe's will by cutting and stealing wood. When tribal residents unloaded their wagon and forced the men to leave, the state responded by siding with the intruders. Apess and a few other men were arrested, charged with "riot, assault, and trespass," and sentenced to thirty days in jail. Massachusetts governor Levi Lincoln threatened to muster the state militia if the tribe continued its resistance, and the white press, perhaps angling for military intervention such as Andrew Jackson's use of the army to enforce the Removal Act in the Southeast, began to call the unfolding crisis the "Woodlot War."

The Mashpee tribe did not meet such hostility and provocation with violence, but neither did they back down from their protests and demands for inclusion and equality. As Apess would later write in his book, *Indian Nullification of the Unconstitutional Laws of Massachusetts, Relative to the Mashpee Tribe; or, The Pretended Riot Explained* (1835), "All that the Indians want in Mashpee is to enjoy their rights without molestation. They have hurt or harmed no one. They have only been searching out their rights, and in so doing, exposed and uncovered, have thrown aside the mantle of deception, that honest men might behold and see for themselves their wrongs." That sentence's final clause is particularly important, for as Apess argues in his book's conclusion, the success of the Mashpee Revolt (as it would come to be known) depended on garnering more sympathetic and inclusive responses from powerful potential allies in the state: "It was necessary, for their future welfare, as it depends in no small degree upon the good opinion of their white brethren, to state the real truth of the case, which could not be done in gentle terms."

Fortunately, the petition and protests, as well as the continued activism of Apess (after his release from jail) and others, did find such sympathetic and inclusive audiences. A first step was securing a friendly journalistic voice to counter the exclusionary press narratives, and Apess found one in William Hallett, editor of the *Boston Advocate* and a rising star in the state's Anti-Masonic Party. His editorial advocacy helped convince the state legislature to send a delegation in late 1833 to investigate conditions in Mashpee, and they produced a lengthy report indicting the white overseers and supporting the tribe's positions. On January 21, 1834, Apess and other tribal leaders journeyed to Boston to address a special evening session of the legislature, and four days later the abolitionist activist and journalist William Lloyd Garrison took up the cause in an editorial in his newspaper, *The Liberator*.

On March 31, 1834, the tribe won a crucial victory: the legislature voted to abolish the community's white guardianship (and with it the overseers) and turn the community into a "district," giving its residents the official power to elect their own government and manage their own affairs. At one and the same time this step granted the Mashpee tribe the sovereignty for which it had been fighting, yet also recognized it as a community much like other self-governing Massachusetts towns; indeed, Mashpee would be incorporated as a town in 1870. While that might seem like a difficult and even contradictory balance to maintain, I would argue instead that it represents an ideal way to navigate the combination of tribal autonomy and inclusive American presence at the heart of Native American history and community in the nineteenth century and into our own moment. The Mashpee won that independent and inclusive balance amidst the exclusionary removal era and offered a vital alternative in the process, and they did so using their own voices and histories, media and political allies, and the language and ideals of the state's and nation's laws.

The Mashpee also relied for that victory on the efforts, presence, and voice of a singular and impressive figure, William Apess. Histories such as Indian Removal and the resistance to it are in many ways communal, yet certain prominent individuals can nonetheless serve as embodiments of those histories and their periods. If Andrew Jackson came to embody the white supremacist and exclusionary attitudes of Indian Removal (and behind it "Indian killing"), then William Apess can be said to embody an alternative, inclusive vision of Native American and American identity and community in this era. In his too brief life, Apess rose up from personal tragedies and darkness to serve as both a model of a cross-cultural American identity and a beacon of hope for fellow Native Americans. In his essays and speeches, such as the angry and impassioned "An Indian's Looking-Glass for the White Man" (1833) and the revisionist and inspiring "Eulogy on King Philip" (1836), he laid out the challenges and possibilities of such an inclusive national community.

Apess wrote at length about his life and identity in his autobiography, *A Son of the Forest* (1829), generally considered the first book-length personal narrative in English by a Native American and well worth reading in full. Yet even a brief sketch of that life here can make clear its connection to both the harshest sides of early-nineteenth-century Native American experience and the manifold ways that Apess transcended them. Per both his own telling and what biographers have since discovered, Apess was born in 1798 into extreme poverty in Colrain, Massachusetts, his parents a Pequot mother and mixed-race (Pequot and English) father. At the age of five his parents separated and abandoned him and his four siblings, and the children went to live with their maternal grandparents, both of whom were apparently alcoholic and abusive. Due to that abuse the children were removed by town selectmen from their grandparents' care, and Apess—still only around five or six years old—became an indentured servant for a local white family. He would remain indentured until he was fifteen years old, the same period in which he himself became addicted to alcohol. He would struggle with that addiction for the rest of his life, with the cerebral hemorrhage that killed him at the age of forty-one usually considered its final destructive effect.

Yet despite those extremely harsh beginnings and tragic effects, Apess lived an impressive and inspiring life that modeled cross-cultural and inclusive American identities at every turn. That began when he ran away from indenture at fifteen, as he joined a New York militia and fought for the United States during the Canadian campaign of the War of 1812. When he returned home around 1818, he joined the Pequot community in Massachusetts, married fellow mixed-race community member Mary Wood, was baptized as a Methodist, and began his career as a preacher. He found the orthodox Methodist Episcopal Church too hierarchical and traditional, and so in 1829 he converted to the more democratic and progressive Protestant Methodist wing, which aided him in his work as a traveling preacher. For the next decade he would travel and preach throughout New England, speaking to both native and non-native congregations, preaching in both Wampanoag and English, and crossing frequently between indigenous communities such as Mashpee and multicultural communities such as Boston. If that life story and ministerial work were all we knew of Apess, he would already serve as a model for inclusive New England and American communities.

But Apess also wrote and spoke in other genres than the personal narrative and the sermon, and in his two best pieces—one an essay appended to a religious collection, the other a speech delivered in the heart of Boston—he argued for such inclusive communities as eloquently and passionately as any American writer ever has. The essay "An Indian's Looking-Glass for the White Man" was first published as an epilogue to *The Experiences of Five Christian Indians of the Pequot Tribe* (1833), a collection of religious conversion narratives edited by Apess, and many of the essay's most striking arguments for inclusion are closely tied to religion. That begins with its not quite grammatical but conversational and entirely compelling opening sentence, "Having a desire to place a few things before my fellow creatures who are traveling with me to the grave, and to that God who is the maker and preserver both of the white man and the Indian, whose abilities are the same, and who are to be judged by one God, who will show no favor to outward appearances, but will judge righteousness."

Apess follows that opening by highlighting and challenging discrimination and mistreatment on a number of levels, but he consistently links those illustrations and arguments back to his inclusive vision of human religion and spirituality. That vision is never more progressive nor more potent than in this moment: "If black or red skins, or any other skin of color is disgraceful to God, it appears that he has disgraced himself a great deal—for he has made fifteen colored people to one white, and placed them here upon this earth." And Apess links that argument for global diversity and equality to a revisionist portrayal of Jesus himself, arguing, "Did you ever hear or read of Christ teaching his disciples that they ought to despise one because his skin was different from theirs? Jesus Christ being a Jew, and those of his Apostles certainly were not whites—and did not he who completed the plan of salvation complete it for the whites as well as for the Jews, and others?" Here we get a glimpse into Apess the itinerant preacher, ministering with no distinctions nor hierarchies to ethnically mixed and cross-cultural congregations.

Much of "Looking-Glass" is thus focused on contexts of religious and human inclusion and equality far beyond any particular nation, but the essay concludes with a final line that sums up the stakes of these ideas and arguments for American identity and ideals: "Do not get tired, ye noble-hearted—only think how many poor Indians want their wounds done up daily; the Lord will reward you, and pray you stop not 'til this tree of distinction shall be leveled to the earth, and the mantle of prejudice torn from every American heart—then shall peace pervade the Union." In this vision of an American community, it is through—and only through—the moves toward such an inclusive identity, one where civic society parallels and complements the egalitarian world spirituality Apess describes, that the nation can move closer to both the Revolution's founding ideals and the exemplary image of a city on a hill.

Truly making that move would also depend on creating a more inclusive narrative of American history, however, and in his speech, "Eulogy on King Philip," Apess narrated precisely such an alternative, inclusive history. Apess claimed the seventeenth-century Wampanoag chief (again, also known as Metacomet) as a maternal ancestor, and on January 26, 1836, he delivered a memorial tribute to Philip at Boston's Odeon lecture hall. It's difficult to overstate the boldness of Apess tackling this subject in this space. The newly opened Odeon would host some of the most prominent American voices of the era, speaking on some of the period's most popular historical and philosophical topics: Supreme Court Justice Joseph Story on Chief Justice John Marshall's life and legacy; popular minister William Ellery Channing on Unitarianism; Ralph Waldo Emerson on transcendentalism; and more. And into that space came Apess to deliver a tribute not only to a Wampanoag leader, but to the man after whom the seventeenth century's most violent and destructive American war had been named. This was a painful Massachusetts history rivaled only by the Salem Witch Trials, and Apess came to the Odeon to praise its principal adversary (as seen from the English perspective at least).

Apess tackles that striking choice and setting immediately and potently, in a paragraph well worth quoting in full:

Yet those purer virtues remain untold. Those noble traits that marked the wild man's course lie buried in the shades of night; and who shall stand? I appeal to the lovers of liberty. But those few remaining descendants who now remain as the monument of the cruelty of those who came to improve our race and correct our errors—and as the immortal Washington lives endeared and engraven on the hearts of every white in America, never to be forgotten in time— even such is the immortal Philip honored, as held in memory by the degraded but yet grateful descendants who appreciate his character; so will every patriot, especially in this enlightened age, respect the rude yet all accomplished son of the forest, that died a martyr to his cause, though unsuccessful, yet as glorious as the American Revolution. Where, then, shall we place the hero of the wilderness?

The untold history that Apess seeks to provide here is thus no less than an alternative vision of the American founding and Revolution, one that would not replace "the immortal Washington" but would complement him with "the immortal Philip" as a revolutionary hero in his own right. Moreover, Apess argues that it is precisely the most idealized American qualities of his audience—"the lovers of liberty," "every patriot"—that will allow them to hear and connect with this inclusive historical revision and narrative.

What follows is an extended, and impressively nuanced, account of both Philip's own life and its cultural and historical contexts. But before he concludes, Apess once again makes clear the purpose for his oration and the contemporary social and political stakes of the inclusive vision for which he has argued: "I say, then, a different course must be pursued, and different laws must be enacted, and all men must operate under one general law. And while you ask yourselves, 'What do they, the Indians, want?' you have only to look at the unjust laws made for them and say, 'They want what I want,' in order to make men of them, good and wholesome citizens." As Apess proved time and again, in his own tragic but inspiring life and in his activism on behalf of a community like Mashpee, an inclusive America governed by such shared goals and equitable laws could welcome and celebrate, rather than remove and exclude, its native citizens and communities.

William Apess died five years after delivering "Eulogy"; while the self-sufficient and sovereign Mashpee community he had helped create persevered successfully, most of the period's other Native American cultures suffered their own tragic and enduring losses. Andrew Jackson and his allies didn't just shift the federal government's policy toward indigenous communities: Indian Removal would become and remain a dominant, exclusionary vision of American identity for well more than a century. Indeed, its legacies continue to this day in the frequent governmental and corporate abuses toward and land thefts from Native American communities, unfolding exclusionary histories exemplified by the infamous incursion of the Dakota Access

Pipeline and its law enforcement allies onto North Dakota's Standing Rock Sioux Reservation in 2016.

Yet the legacies of Apess, the Mashpee, the Cherokee Memorials, and their allies endured as well. Their voices found echoes in the late-nineteenth-century speaking tours and activisms of figures such as the Ponca Chief Standing Bear and the Paiute writer Sarah Winnemucca. Their calls for legal and political equality helped inspire Nipo Strongheart and other indigenous performers and artists whose tireless efforts yielded the 1924 Indian Citizenship Act. Their revisionist and alternative visions of history and spirituality were carried forward by both the American Indian Movement and the Native American Renaissance authors of the 1960s and 1970s. And their resistance to exclusionary laws and demands for inclusion in our national conversations and communities likewise motivate the protesters at Standing Rock, who continue to fight for an America with William Apess, not Andrew Jackson, as its embodiment.

Chapter Four

Mexican Americans Have Never Left

The Mexican-American War (1846–1848) was linked specifically and on multiple levels to white supremacist and exclusionary definitions of American communities and identity. The first step in the decade-long build-up to the war was Texas's March 2, 1836, declaration of independence from Mexico, which took place in large part because Anglo American settlers in the Mexican province (led by Stephen F. Austin, who brought the first 300 Anglo American families to the region in 1825) wished to practice the system of African American chattel slavery and could not do so while part of Mexico (which had abolished slavery in much of the nation in 1829 and in Texas in 1830). After a few months of bloody conflict, including the infamous March 6th Battle of the Alamo and the subsequent Texan victory at the April 21th Battle of San Jacinto, Mexican president Antonio López de Santa Anna surrendered on May 14, 1836, signing the Treaty of Velasco that recognized Texas as an independent republic, one which would feature slavery as a core element throughout its brief period of existence.

Pro-slavery forces in the U.S. government sought to annex Texas immediately; the Whigs and other anti-slavery voices resisted for nearly a decade, but in December 1845 the United States annexed Texas and made it the nation's twenty-eighth state. At the same time, the newly elected democratic president, James Polk, himself a slave owner and a strong advocate of expanding the territorial reach of the slave-holding Southern states in particular, was seeking to purchase additional land from Mexico and to set the border between the two nations significantly farther south, at the Rio Grande. When Mexico refused these offers, Polk disregarded Mexican sovereignty and borders, moving U.S. troops (commanded by future president Zachary Taylor) into the Mexican region known as the Nueces Strip. Further west, Polk sent explorer John Frémont and a group of armed men into the Mexican province of Alta California, where Frémont built a fort on Gavilan Peak and raised the American flag over it. Mexico responded predictably to these overt intrusions into its territories, moving its own forces into the disputed regions and skirmishing there with U.S. troops, and the war between the two nations began, one that would last more than two years and culminate in a U.S. victory and the February 1848 Treaty of Guadalupe Hidalgo.

The war may have had those controversial and, in many ways, overtly white supremacist and exclusionary contexts, but the question of what would happen to Mexican Americans in the war's aftermath was as of 1848 an entirely open and potentially inclusive one. The treaty set the U.S.-Mexico border at the Rio Grande, and in so doing ceded a vast swath of Mexican territory to the United States—not only the disputed Nueces region in southern Texas, but also the much larger provinces of Santa Fe de Nuevo, México (which became the Southwestern U.S. territories), and Alta California (which became California). There were, of course, numerous Mexican citizens living in those regions, in communities that had in many cases existed for well more than 150 years by this time, and the terms of the treaty respected their presence and rights in a number of crucial ways: Article VIII promised that they would be "free to continue where they now reside, . . . retaining the property which they possess in the said territories," their right to which would be "inviolably respected"; the same Article gave all those Mexican citizens the chance to "acquire the title and rights of citizens of the United States" if they chose, and indeed noted that those who stayed in the territories for longer than a year "shall be considered to have elected to become citizens of the United States"; and Article IX likewise guaranteed that these new Mexican Americans would be "secured in the free exercise of their religion without restriction."

Yet if the Treaty of Guadalupe Hidalgo thus in many ways reflected an inclusive vision of these longstanding communities and their newfound status as part of the expanding United States, subsequent realities too often comprised precisely the opposite. Over the next few decades, a number of factors conspired to dispossess many Mexican landowners, destroy many of these existing communities, and displace many Mexican Americans in favor of arriving Anglo American settlers. Perhaps the single most striking such force was the discovery of gold at Sutter's Mill in California in January 1848 (just weeks before the treaty's signing), a historical event which would, in the course of the seven-year gold rush, bring more than 300,000 settlers (from the United States and elsewhere) to the region. Within two years, in fact, California's Spanish-speaking community numbered only 15 percent of its population. But while the gold rush certainly offered a particularly clear rationale for migration to California and other western territories, the truth is that many of these settlers came in search of more than just quick riches: land was in many ways an even more valuable commodity (particularly given the industrialization and development of the Eastern United States throughout this same period), and in order to get it Anglo American arrivals often took part in the illegal but frustratingly successful practice of squatting. These squatters would simply occupy land owned by Mexican Americans and begin to live on and work it, trusting that the U.S. government and laws would reward them with eventual property rights to that land.

Despite the treaty's guarantees, far too often the United States did indeed side with these squatters and others who imposed upon and attacked Mexican American homes and communities. The most overt such moment was the so-called Squatters' riot of August 1850, in which the rapidly changing California community of Sacramento became dominated by arriving squatters with whose "natural" land claims much of the legal and governmental system sided, bolstered by many popular media voices and narratives. Indeed, one of the squatter leaders, James McClatchy, even created a newspaper, the *Settlers and Miners Tribune*, to amplify those pro-squatter narratives; he would later found the *Sacramento Bee* (which remains in operation to this day) to further advance these claims. While those Sacramento events represented an extreme effect of squatting, the practice took place throughout the newly acquired territories in these years, and was frequently (if not consistently) supported by the U.S. authorities. Most strikingly, the California Land Act of 1851 (a U.S. congressional federal law) provided legal cover for Anglo squatting, forcing Mexican landowners to verify the legitimacy of their titles (requiring documents that many such landowners, whose families had occupied the land for generations, simply did not have) and returning any land not so verified to the public domain.

Complementing these social and legal protections for Anglo American squatters were laws designed to limit the rights of existing Mexican American communities (among other non-Anglo minorities). The Foreign Miners' Tax of 1850, for example, imposed an outrageous $20 per month tax for "foreign miners" seeking to work in California, with "foreign" defined overtly as any resident who was not a "free white person"; pro-immigrant governor John McDougall repealed the law in 1851, but his successor created a Foreign Miners' License Tax, which reinstated and carried forward for decades this practice of segregating access to this central California industry. (These taxes were likewise directed at the Chinese arrivals, whom I discuss in chapter 5.) Even more overt and discriminatory was California's Anti-Vagrancy Act of 1855, also known as the Greaser Act because its second section explicitly linked the "vagrants, vagabonds, and dangerous and suspicious persons" it targeted to "all persons who are commonly known as 'Greasers' or the issue of Spanish and Indian blood." Discriminatory and white supremacist laws such as these both reflected and helped extend the period's widespread illegal oppressions and violence directed at Mexican

American communities, not only in the form of squatting but also lynchings, mob violence, and many other exclusionary treatments.

Taken together, those decades of illegal and legal, violent and official oppressions of Mexican Americans fundamentally distorted the promises and vision of the Treaty of Guadalupe Hidalgo. Had the treaty been enacted and enforced as written, had these Mexican American communities been able to enter the United States with the full rights and sovereignty guaranteed there, it would be impossible for any twenty-first-century definition of American identity not to include such longstanding and foundational Hispanic presences as a core element. Exclusionary narratives of "English only" as a national language, for example, would be far less easily argued for had these Spanish-speaking Mexican American communities retained their full legal status. Yet instead, numerous factors in the treaty's aftermath worked together to displace Mexican Americans from their land, their rights, and too often their very presence within the expanding United States.

So these longstanding Mexican American communities were threatened, oppressed, and often dispossessed and displaced in the decades after the Treaty of Guadalupe Hidalgo. During the same period, and in direct relationship to those unfolding histories, collective memories and national narratives often defined the Hispanic American presence in the United States in overtly exclusionary ways. That presence was a far older one than that of any other European culture or community in America, with a continually occupied city like Florida's St. Augustine having been settled by Spanish arrivals in 1565, nearly half a century before the English arrived in Jamestown. Yet in the terms of these exclusionary narratives, Hispanic communities constituted part of the prior history of these American territories, thus rendering them fundamentally outside of and foreign to the new and evolving, overtly non-Hispanic "American" communities in these places.

One way to challenge those narratives and argue for an alternative, inclusive vision of these places, and of America through them, is to note that numerous Hispanic and Mexican American communities did not go anywhere, resisting these oppressions and exclusions, remaining part of these changing American spaces, and evolving with them in the decades and now centuries beyond the treaty. That's true of St. Augustine, to this day the longest continually occupied European American community and one that features sites and monuments that foreground that Hispanic American heritage and presence, including statues to Juan Ponce de Léon (the region's first Spanish explorer), Pedro Menéndez (the city's founder), and Father Pedro Camps (the spiritual leader of one of the city's most significant Hispanic immigrant communities, the Minorcans). But it's also and even more tellingly true of many spaces within the Treaty of Guadalupe Hidalgo's purview, including both the Tejano community of South Texas and the Old Town community in San Diego.

Spanish explorers began to reach the area that would come to be known as Texas in the late-seventeenth century, and as early as 1731 permanent arrivals settled at the Presidio San Antonio de Bexar (modern-day San Antonio). During the course of the eighteenth century, additional Spanish settlements would spread out across the region, featuring distinct cultural heritages (such as Isleños from the Canary Islands) but linked by the evolving communal identity known as Tejano. Indeed, that communal identity grew strong enough that, while the Tejanos were certainly still part of first New Spain and then (after the end of the Mexican War of Independence in 1821) Mexico, there were various moments and moves toward establishing a separate Tejano state, one less directly tied to those larger colonial and national entities. That more independent identity was directly linked to the early 1820s invitation to outside settlers to move into and help further develop the region, an invitation that by 1830 would bring some 30,000 arrivals from (largely) the United States. While tensions between those largely English-speaking settlers and the Mexican government would help precipitate the 1836 Texan revolt and war, the relationship between the new settlers (who came to be called Texians) and the Tejanos was complex but much less overtly hostile, and certainly most of the Tejanos seem to have remained in the region during the era of the independent Republic of Texas.

The majority of Tejanos likewise remained in the region after the Treaty of Guadalupe Hidalgo, becoming part of South Texas and the expanding United States. Indeed, the area's truly multicultural community—which across the remainder of the nineteenth century would come to include sizeable groups of Irish, Dutch, Polish, and Czech immigrants, among many other cultures—became part of an evolving Tejano identity, one that incorporated these various influences into distinct combinatory features. Perhaps the most famous such feature is "Tex-Mex" cuisine, a culinary tradition quite distinct from either traditional Mexican food or more Texan/Southern items like barbecue. But in many other cultural and social arenas, from music to literature to a particular shared accent, the Tejano community has evolved and endured in South Texas. The late-twentieth-century writer and scholar Gloria Anzaldúa, one of the most famous descendants of the original Tejano settlers, offers a nuanced and critical but also celebratory vision of Tejano heritage and identity in her book *Borderlands/La Frontera: The New Mestiza* (1987), an autoethnographic work that both highlights and incorporates multiculturalism and multilingualism as essential elements of this unique but (Anzaldúa argues, and I would agree) exemplary American community.

Equally longstanding, enduring, and exemplary is another of the nation's oldest Hispanic (and indeed European) American settlements, the Old Town community in San Diego. San Diego is considered the first West Coast site to

be explored by Europeans, with the Castilian Spanish explorer Juan Rodri-
guez Cabrillo reaching the bay as early as 1542. The first permanent Spanish
settlement in Alta California, was likewise located in San Diego, as groups
from New Spain's Baja California (the Yucatán peninsula in modern-day
Mexico) reached the area by both land and sea in 1769, establishing both the
Presidio (fort) and the San Diego de Alcalá Mission in the city. Over the next
half-century the city would develop into the spiritual and social capital of
Alta California, and after Mexico won its independence from Spain in 1821,
San Diego's residents petitioned successfully to become a pueblo, a form of
official status within the Mexican nation that elevated the community's significance one step further (bringing with it the new municipal leadership
position of an alcalde, with Juan María Osuna elected as the first). But
population changes and emigrations led the city to lose that status in 1838,
meaning that, as was the case with the Tejanos, in many ways San Diego
welcomed the influx of Anglo and other American arrivals around the time
of the Mexican American War, as these new settlers helped the city evolve
into its new, multicultural, mid-nineteenth-century form.

That influx, and the aftermath of the war and the Treaty of Guadalupe
Hidalgo, was not without its complications and conflicts, of course. But as
was the case in South Texas, the story of San Diego post-treaty seems to have
been more one of combination and collective evolution than of competition
or displacement. Old Town came to be known as such precisely because it
endured as part of the new American city, one complemented by new development closer to the bay in the area known initially as New San Diego and
later as New Town. The city's final alcalde, trader and saloon-owner Joshua
Bean, was elected its first mayor after the city was incorporated by the
California State Legislature in 1850. While Bean was an Anglo American
settler who had come to the city after the Mexican American War, his joint
role as businessman and political leader was paralleled by similar figures
from the city's Mexican American community, including prominent ranchers
such as Jose Antonia Altamirano (who fought with the Americans during the
Mexican American War) and Doña Josefa Felipa Osuna de Marron (whose
family sided with the Mexicans but who famously returned to the city after
the war and remained on her ranch throughout the nineteenth century). Figures and stories like these are memorialized throughout San Diego's Old
Town, not only because they are part of its history and heritage but also and
especially because they represent a Mexican American presence and influence that have continued throughout the 170 years since the treaty and endure into the community's and city's twenty-first-century identities.

The fundamental, longstanding, and enduring truth of communities like
San Diego, the Texas Tejano region and culture (and indeed all of Texas), St.
Augustine, and so many more is one of addition, not change. Certainly the
power structure of these cities and regions changed hands after the Mexican

American War and the Treaty of Guadalupe Hidalgo, which meant that most of their official features—laws and government, the language of public spaces and conversations, and so on—reflected an Anglo American–dominated society. But even if we were inclined to equate those official elements with the whole of a community (and I don't believe we do so in the context of any other American community), to focus our collective narratives or memories on this Anglo American presence in the post-treaty era is to do two troubling and inaccurate things. First, it reinforces the post-treaty thefts, dispossessions, and oppressions of Mexican Americans, turning those illegal and exclusionary tactics into defining histories rather than the shameful and hateful abuses they were. And second, it substitutes those exclusionary histories for the longstanding and evolving identities and legacies of places that have in fact comprised some of our most inclusive American communities, ones that even before the treaty featured multiple cultures, languages, and presences and that in the centuries since have continued to do so under the United States flag.

One important and inspiring way for us collectively to better remember those histories and communities would be to highlight and read late-nineteenth and early-twentieth-century Mexican American authors, literary figures who gave voice to these stories in their writings and who in their lives and identities embodied the continued presence of Hispanic Americans within and beyond the turn-of-the-century United States. While there were certainly many such authors who wrote and published in Spanish throughout (as well as after) the pre-treaty era, it is the first Mexican American authors to publish in English whose works, voices, and lives especially exemplify this additive, combinatory, multicultural and multilingual community as it evolved in the post-treaty decades.

To date, the most famous nineteenth-century Mexican American literary figures are two who were created (or at least popularized) by non-Hispanic authors: Joaquin Murieta, the legendary (and perhaps imaginary) "Robin Hood of El Dorado" made famous by Cherokee novelist John Rollin Ridge in his bestselling book *The Life and Adventures of Joaquin Murieta: The Celebrated California Bandit* (1854); and Ramona, the beautiful, tragic, mixed-race heroine and social reformer Helen Hunt Jackson's hugely successful historical novel *Ramona* (1884). Both of those books and characters are connected to complex and important Mexican American and American histories, and both have a great deal to tell us about those histories and these communities: Murieta in his willingness to resist both Anglo oppression and U.S. law in a quest for vengeance and justice; and Ramona in the multilayered, interconnected, and equally endangered histories of the Mexican haciendas, Spanish missions, and Native American communities through which her story moves. But both these characters and stories are deeply romanticized, perhaps in part due to their authors' status as interested outsiders to these Mexican American communities and histories, and in any case, we can and should go beyond them, to recover and read long-forgotten Mexican American literary voices like María Amparo Ruiz de Burton (1832–1895) and María Cristina Mena (1893–1965).

María Amparo Ruiz de Burton's striking nineteenth-century life spanned and linked both Mexico and the United States and the pre– and post–Treaty of Guadalupe Hidalgo eras, not only geographically and chronologically but through a series of complex and telling moments and themes. She was born in July 1832 in Baja California, the granddaughter of Jose Manuel Ruiz, a former regional governor turned Mexican military commander; his brother Francisco, her great-uncle, commanded the Presidio of San Diego in Alta California during the same period. When María was fifteen years old, U.S. troops conquered her hometown of La Paz as part of the Mexican American War, and María met and fell in love with a member of those U.S. forces, Captain Henry Burton of the 1st Regiment of New York Volunteers. Burton and his regiment remained in Baja California through the war's end, and after the Treaty of Guadalupe Hidalgo he encouraged María and her family, and other residents of Baja California, to move to Alta California, and pursue the opportunity to become U.S. citizens; María, her mother, and brother moved to Monterey in order to do so. Less than a year later, just after her seventeenth birthday, and in the face of opposition from both the Catholic Church and the new Anglo American authorities in the territory, María married Burton.

Over the next decade María and Henry would build a multifaceted family and life together in this evolving, multicultural Southern California community. Henry was made commander of the army post at the Mission San Diego de Alcalá, and the couple bought a nearby ranch, Rancho Jamul, which they worked for the next few years alongside María's brother and mother. María had two children during this period, a daughter Nellie in 1850 and a son Henry in 1854, and also pursued her nascent literary ambitions, starting a small San Diego theatre company in which both soldiers and civilians performed. But the family's life and trajectory shifted significantly in the buildup to the Civil War: Henry was ordered back east to Fort Monroe, Virginia, in 1859, and would never return to California; he served as brigadier general during the Civil War, contracted malaria during the long 1864–1865 siege of Petersburg (Virginia), and died of complications from the illness in April 1869, leaving María a thirty-seven-year-old widow and single mother to two teenage children.

Ruiz de Burton (as I'll call her from now on) and her children returned to California after Henry's death but found that their ownership of Rancho Jamul was in doubt, contested by various Anglo squatters and claimants. Ruiz de Burton refused to yield this family home and business to such interlopers without a fight, and would spend much of the next few decades in legal and financial battles to prove, secure, and maintain her claim to the ranch (or, more exactly, her late husband's claim, since both as a woman and as a Mexican American her claim was even more tenuous than his). She even traveled back east, lobbying contacts in Washington, DC, and finally succeeding at securing a land patent in her and her children's names on October 26, 1876. The patent did not end either the threat of squatting or the ongoing legal battles, but it nonetheless reflected Ruiz de Burton's steadfast desire and ability to fight not only for this particular 9,000 acres of Southern California land, but also for her presence and status within that American community.

For Ruiz de Burton, that fight was not only for her own land and legacy, but for her broader cultural community. As she wrote to her longtime friend and English tutor, Mariano Vallejo, "I am persuaded that we were born to do something more than simply live, that is, we were born for something more, for the rest of our poor countrymen." While her multidecade legal efforts certainly served as a model for such communal activism, it was in her two published works of socially realistic fiction that she truly portrayed and advocated for her Mexican American compatriots, in contrast to widely accepted narratives of Californian and American identity that sought to avoid and displace this community. Just as importantly, she wrote and published these novels in English, making her the first Mexican American to do so and further embodying the bilingual and multicultural identity that she (and her mother and brother), her husband, and her children had created throughout these decades.

The first of those two novels, *Who Would Have Thought It?* (1872), published by the Philadelphia press J.B. Lippincott with no author's name on the title page (but registered at the Library of Congress to Mrs. Henry S. Burton), offers a bitingly sarcastic portrayal of Northeastern U.S. abolitionists, Congregationalists, Boston Brahmins, and other longstanding American communities. Ruiz de Burton's heroine, Lola, is a Mexican American orphan who has been raised by Native Americans and finds herself adopted into a prominent progressive family, only to face racial and ethnic, gender, religious, and other prejudices. Putting this strikingly cross-cultural character in conversation and contrast with so many iconic American identities—even Abraham Lincoln himself comes under fire in the course of the novel's satirical arc—allows Ruiz de Burton's narrator and novel to ask the title question not only of accepted narratives of American exceptionalism and ideals, but also of who is and is not considered part of that American community at all. The novel's final sentence, addressed to one character but with a much broader range of meanings, ends, "and you know it, and so does the nation"—but *Who Would Have Thought It?* makes clear that there is much the nation does not know about both its histories and its present community.

Ruiz de Burton did not publish her second novel for thirteen years (she was busy with her legal battles, and did find time to adapt *Don Quixote* into a five-act comic stage play during this period), but it was well worth the wait. *The Squatter and the Don: A Novel Descriptive of Contemporary Occurrences in California* (1885) was published in San Francisco under the pseudonym C. Loyal, a bilingual play on the phrases "Ciudadano Leal" and "Loyal Citizen," each used proudly by Mexican Americans to capture their dual national allegiances. The novel covers roughly the thirteen years between 1872 and 1885 in the lives of two representative families: the Darrells (the titular Squatter and his family, who have migrated to California to make a new life after failures back east) and the Alamars (the titular Don and his family, who find their longstanding California ranch under assault from such squatters and their many allies), legal and cultural opponents who find themselves linked by the controversial, cross-cultural romance between two of their children.

Ruiz de Burton works to do justice to the multilayered perspectives and stories of both families and their cultures, as illustrated by the book's first two chapters: "Squatter Darrell Reviews the Past," in which William and Mary Darrell debate not only the circumstances that have brought them to this point but the very nature of their intrusion into California (with William arguing that they are "settlers" and Mary countering that he "must accept the epithet of 'Squatter'"); and "The Don's View of the Treaty of Guadalupe Hidalgo," in which Don Mariano Alamar expounds upon that historical moment and, especially, the decades of illegal and legal mistreatment and oppression that have followed for his home, family, and community. The narrator likewise parallels the two chapters, noting, "The law of necessity made the Squatter and the Don, distant as they were—distant in every way, without reckoning the miles between them—talk quite warmly of the same matter. The point of view was of course different, for how could it be otherwise?" And in the course of the novel, both the fictional cross-cultural romance and the historical schemes of railroad corporations and the U.S. government serve to bridge that distance, bringing the Squatter and the Don into a hesitant but definite shared understanding in the Californian and American community.

Ruiz de Burton ends her novel with a "Conclusion—Out with the Invader," in which she moves away from the fictional families entirely to make an impassioned plea on behalf of her own such community. That "invader," to be clear, is not Anglo American settlers nor even squatters (with whose situation the novel has largely sympathized), but rather "the monopoly," a conglomerate of corporate and governmental interests that Ruiz de Burton in her concluding paragraph argues has long thwarted "the will of the people" in California (and elsewhere). That concluding phrase itself highlights Ruiz de Burton's vision of a multicultural Californian and American "people," one not without its foundational distances but with the potential to be as united as these two fictional families have become through the novel's romance plot (and indeed its very title). In her groundbreaking fiction, as in her inspiring life and activism, Ruiz de Burton reflected those frustrating distances but modeled that potential for a unified American community beyond them.

Born in Mexico City in April 1893, just two years before Ruiz de Burton passed away (in Chicago, fighting her legal and land battles until the end), María Cristina Mena experienced her own distinct versions of a Mexican American identity, a cross-cultural marriage, and a multifaceted and multi-genre literary career. Even before her parents sent her to New York City at the age of fourteen (to escape the imminent Mexican Revolution), Mena experienced multiple educational, cultural, religious, and linguistic settings, from a Catholic convent school in Mexico City to a boarding school in England. Once in New York, Mena built upon those various influences to launch an impressively early and groundbreaking literary career: she published her first two short stories at the age of twenty: "The Gold Vanity Set" in *American* magazine and "John of God, the Water-Carrier" in *Century* magazine, making her the first Mexican American woman writer to appear in such periodicals. She would publish seven more stories in *Century* between 1914 and 1916, most, like her first two, featuring Mexican characters and communities coming into complex contact with indigenous peoples, American tourists, and other early-twentieth-century cross-cultural and hemispheric forces.

Mena's stories consistently occupy an uneasy space between stereotype and resistance, utilizing (and perhaps perpetuating) various widespread perceptions of Mexican and indigenous communities yet at the same time offering readers more nuanced depictions of those identities and worlds. Similarly, her stories seem at times to depict women as beautiful objects, but at the same time she complicates and challenges those images, particularly through plot devices that focus on the era's new plastic surgery techniques and procedures (often brought from the United States to Mexico, and thus representing as well one more layer of cross-cultural migration and combination). "The Vine-Leaf" (*Century*, December 1914), perhaps Mena's best story, exemplifies these and other ambiguities, as its protagonist, a prominent Mexico City physician, tells a young female patient the story of his first patient, a mysterious "Marquésa" for whom he performed a plastic surgery procedure to remove the titular birthmark. That procedure, and the changes it helped enact, seem to have allowed the Marquésa to get away with murder and make a new life for herself outside of her existing cultural and gendered categories, making her at once a dangerous femme fatale and a woman with agency and power in an era that would seek to limit them.

Despite these complexities, Mena's stories were often perceived as simply offering sentimental local color depictions of Mexico for curious American audiences (tourists, we might say); indeed, her *Century* editors themselves pushed her to produce more stories of that type. Partially in response to those pressures, and also to reflect the diversity of both Mexican American culture and her own interests, Mena wrote her only nonfiction essay for the *Century*: "Julián Carillo: The Herald of a Musical Monroe Doctrine" (1915). Through "offering the public an account of the movement with which *Maestro* Julián Carillo has already captured the imagination of a growing circle of musical artists in New York," as she writes in her first paragraph, Mena at the same time develops her titular thesis of Carillo's "Musical Monroe Doctrine," a new vision of hemispheric American identity in which both Carillo and Mena herself can occupy a far more central role than simply as picturesque locals for tourists to encounter. She comes in her concluding sentence to her fullest vision of that emerging new collective identity, writing, "I wish I had room to tell of the enthusiasm of those artists, men of note from the Metropolitan Opera and other important orchestras, who have abandoned excellent engagements to enroll themselves under this ruddy-brown American of the aboriginal breed, whose day-dream of patriotism embraces the Western Hemisphere."

Just a year later, the twenty-three-year-old Mena would begin her own cross-cultural romance and family, marrying Henry Kellet Chambers, a forty-nine-year-old Australian American journalist and playwright. She would largely put her literary career on hold during the course of their marriage, publishing one final historical short story about the Mexican Revolution, "A Son of the Tropics," in *Household Magazine* in 1931. After Chambers passed away in 1935, Mena (now María Cristina Chambers) returned to writing in a new genre, publishing five children's books about Mexican and Mexican American history and culture between 1942 and 1953. These books cover subjects as wide-ranging as the historical commemorations of *Boy Heroes of Chapultepec: A Story of the Mexican War* (1953) and the contemporary romance of *The Two Eagles* (1943), which translates her interests in images of gender and beauty for young readers. And as with all of her writings, published in English for American readers of all types, these books extend Mena's ideas about the twentieth-century presence and role of Mexican and Mexican American stories and identities, not just as a neighbor to the United States but as an integral part of America's own literary, artistic, and cultural identities.

Writers like Ruiz de Burton and Mena helped ensure not only that Mexican American voices and works would endure as part of the American literary and cultural landscape but also that the post–Treaty of Guadalupe Hidalgo invasions and oppressions would not erase or displace this longstanding and evolving American community. The narratives of Mexican Americans as fundamentally outside of and foreign to American identity likewise endured into the twentieth century, however, as illustrated by Texas congressman John Box's 1928 argument for extending that decade's restrictive, discriminatory Quota Acts to Mexican immigrants. As Box thundered in a speech to the House of Representatives, "Every reason which calls for the exclusion of the most wretched, ignorant, dirty, diseased, and degraded people of Europe or Asia demands that the illiterate, unclean, peonized masses moving this way from Mexico be stopped at the border." In case his division of those stereotypical narratives of Mexicans from idealized images of American identity was not clear enough, he added, "Another purpose of the immigration laws is the protection of American racial stock from further degradation or change through mongrelization."

Contesting such exclusionary images and arguments requires more than literary works and exemplary lives, however compellingly inclusive they might be. To challenge such discriminatory narratives and make the case for full Mexican American citizenship within an American community, national civic and activist organizations are also necessary. And the year after Box's speech saw the founding of the first such national Hispanic American civil rights organization: the League of United Latin American Citizens (LULAC), created in February 1929 in Corpus Christi, Texas. LULAC's initial members came from a few existing, smaller organizations, including El Orden Hijos de America (The Order of the Sons of America), El Orden Caballeros de America (The Order of the Knights of America), and the League of Latino American Citizens. A number of the founding members had also fought in World War I, and LULAC was modeled in part on veterans' organizations, as well as on the National Association for the Advanced of Colored People (NAACP). Two founding members of El Orden Caballeros, Pedro and María Hernández, were particularly instrumental in developing LULAC's multilayered social and political agenda: María, an elementary school teacher and mother of ten, focused on educational outreach and offering support for expectant and new mothers; Pedro, a political and legal activist, helped organize such efforts as a successful lawsuit challenging the Texas legislature's longstanding policy of failing to invite Mexican Americans to serve on juries.

Over the next few decades, LULAC would continue and extend those efforts: creating community education, scholarship, and preschool programs (such as the popular Little School of the 400 early childhood program); conducting voter registration campaigns and opposing poll taxes and other efforts to disenfranchise Hispanic voters; suing Southwestern school districts that practiced racial segregation and denied Mexican American students equal access and opportunities; and in many other ways advocating for both basic rights and full citizenship for Mexican and Hispanic Americans. Two of those successful educational lawsuits, *Mendez v. Westminster* (1945) and *Minerva Delgado v. Bastrop Independent School District* (1948)—which were litigated by LULAC's cadre of volunteer attorneys—helped form the precedents that would lead to the Supreme Court's turning-point anti-segregation decision in *Brown v. Board of Education* (1954).

That successful opposition to educational segregation illustrates the important national role played by an organization like LULAC. LULAC's commitment to supporting assimilation into American culture, complemented by an emphasis on English-language proficiency among other similar elements, didn't always help Mexican and Hispanic Americans express and celebrate their heritages and cultures as fully or proudly as they should. As a result, across the twentieth century, the organization (while still existing to this day) took a gradual and appropriate backseat to others more overtly focused on cultural awareness, understanding, and celebration. One such organization was the National Council of La Raza (NCLR): founded in 1968 as the Southwest Council of the La Raza and renamed in 1973 to reflect its national goals, NCLR (which also endures to this day, now known as UnidosUS) offers Hispanic Americans opportunities to participate in an inclusive American community while commemorating all that embodies their own cultural and ethnic heritages.

But in response to the kinds of exclusionary attitudes and efforts that followed the Treaty of Guadalupe Hidalgo, white supremacist and violent rhetoric still very much present in moments like Box's 1928 speech, there was a significant need for an organization like LULAC, one working to highlight for all Americans just how much Mexican and Hispanic Americans had always been and remained part of broader American histories and identities. This inclusive activism helps us better remember longstanding American communities like the South Texas Tejanos and San Diego's Old Town, makes clear how much authors like María Amparo Ruiz de Burton and María Cristina Mena belong in any narrative of American literary and cultural history, and offers a chance to redeem the Treaty of Guadalupe Hidalgo's promise of full American citizenship and protection for all Mexican Americans.

Chapter Five

Un-American and Unsuccessful Chinese Exclusions

In the mid-to-late nineteenth century, Chinese Americans became the focus of yet another wave of exclusionary, xenophobic paranoia, bigotry, and oppression directed at a particular cultural community. Such targeted exclusionary attitudes had been a recurring pattern for at least a century in America, since Benjamin Franklin's 1751 worry that his adopted home of Pennsylvania, "founded by the *English*, [should] become a colony of aliens, who will shortly be so numerous as to Germanize us instead of our Anglifying them, and will never adopt our language or customs, any more than they can acquire our complexion" (Franklin's emphasis). In post–Revolutionary America such sentiments were directed at the French, as illustrated by the 1793–1794 panic over the presence and potentially subversive actions of French ambassador to the U.S. Edmund-Charles Genêt. In the early decades of the nineteenth century, both Catholics and the Irish (two overlapping but not identical cultural communities) became the target of widespread xenophobic narratives and fears. While these exclusionary waves did at times produce legal and political effects, the forces of inclusion managed to withstand and defeat them in each case: the 1798 Alien and Sedition Acts that unconstitutionally sought to limit Franco American citizenship and civic engagement were allowed to expire in 1800 and 1801; the Know Nothing Party that sought to exclude Irish Americans achieved no significant national electoral victories; and so on.

This exclusionary pattern recurred, but with distinctly and tragically different results, when it came to Chinese Americans in the mid-to-late nineteenth century. Chinese immigrants had been arriving to the West Coast of the continent since at least the late eighteenth century, when the region was still part of New Spain, and were thus a relatively longstanding (if also

relatively small) cultural community by the time Anglo settlers and the United States expanded into the area in the 1830s and 1840s. But significantly
more Chinese immigrants arrived during and after those decades, spurred in
part by the needs of those growing settlements (especially the dangerous
work of creating railroad lines, but also other opportunities for work in these
developing communities) and in part by the internationally prominent and
alluring narratives of the 1849 California Gold Rush. And of course, despite
the area's longstanding Chinese presence (and that of Filipino Americans in
Louisiana, about which I write in the next chapter), most of the Anglo and
other U.S. arrivals to the region were encountering Chinese and Asian
American communities for the first time.

As those initial encounters played out during the 1840s and 1850s, some
of the more xenophobic and vocal U.S. settlers began to develop a bigoted
and fearful set of images of these Chinese American communities. Those
images coalesced into the overarching concept of the "Yellow Peril," a narrative of the various, interconnected threats that these Chinese Americans (both
as existing communities and as potential future arrivals) supposedly posed:
threats of crime and vice (including gambling, prostitution, and drugs);
threats of disease and dirtiness; licentious threats to white women; and more
amorphous but just as potent threats of "otherness," of culture and customs,
religion and race that seemed from this exclusionary perspective fundamentally foreign and even hostile to "American" society. In journalism and political cartoons, in political speeches and campaigns by activist organizations,
and in cultural texts like local color writer Bret Harte's popular song "The
Heathen Chinee," this Yellow Peril narrative became a staple of California
and western society in the mid-nineteenth century.

While that narrative began to develop in the decades before the Civil War,
it was after the war that it truly became a dominant force in not only Californian and western but also national society and politics. The debate over the
1870 Naturalization Act illustrates the era's shift in national exclusionary
narratives quite clearly: the law was overtly intended to make it possible for
African American ex-slaves and their descendants to become U.S. citizens,
and while of course there was some congressional and civic debate over that
concept, it was broadly popular enough for the law to pass easily; yet when
Senator Charles Sumner of Massachusetts sought to extend the law's provisions to Chinese and other Asian American communities, he was met with
widespread opposition. Sumner's proposal to open up the naturalization process for all American arrivals and residents was rejected by Congress, and
the July 1870 Naturalization Act ends instead with the much more specific
phrase, "And be it further enacted, That the naturalization laws are hereby
extended to aliens of African nativity and to persons of African descent."

That wedding of Yellow Peril fears to overtly exclusionary attitudes toward and treatment of Chinese Americans and communities took a number

of prominent forms throughout the 1870s and beyond. In California, the narrative became tied to a popular and influential political movement, one alternatively known as Kearneyism (after Denis Kearney, the firebrand labor leader who was one of the movement's most vocal leaders) and Sandlotism (because Kearney and his ilk held their anti-Chinese rallies in large such lots); new political parties like the Workingmen's Party of California (with its slogan "The Chinese Must Go!") linked their fortunes to this mass movement. Throughout the west, mob and collective violence against Chinese American communities became all too common: from the Los Angeles Chinatown massacre of 1871 to the destruction of Denver's Chinatown in 1880, the 1885 Rock Springs (Wyoming) and 1887 Hells Canyon (Oregon) massacres of Chinese American miners to the mid-1880s destruction and displacement of Chinese American communities in such Northwestern cities as Seattle and Tacoma, such dark histories were repeated time and again during this period. And most lastingly and destructively, the first national immigration laws were created directly out of these exclusionary narratives, laws designed not only to curtail future Chinese arrivals but also to destroy existing Chinese American communities.

The first such national immigration law, the 1875 Page Act, was relatively narrow in its scope, but nonetheless sought to prohibit Chinese women from immigrating, calling them "lewd and immoral" arrivals coming "for the purposes of prostitution"; such a ban itself severely impacted the potential of existing Chinese American communities to grow and develop. And the 1882 Chinese Exclusion Act and its various aftermath provisions and laws fully cemented those dual exclusionary goals. The act made it illegal for nearly all Chinese arrivals to enter the United States (first for a ten-year period, but the 1892 Geary Act extended the ban indefinitely), but it and its many follow-up laws also featured numerous elements designed to affect and ultimately destroy existing Chinese American communities: the Exclusion Act stripped the citizenship from those who had been able to gain it (certain states like Connecticut had allowed Chinese Americans to naturalize as citizens); the 1888 Scott Act made it illegal for most Chinese Americans living in the United States to leave the country and seek to return; and the 1892 Geary Act required all Chinese Americans to carry a "resident permit" at all times or risk immediate arrest and deportation as suspected "illegal aliens."

In a series of late 1880s and 1890s cases, the Supreme Court upheld the Exclusion Act and its follow-ups as legal and constitutional (far from a settled question, since the Constitution does not mention immigration at all, much less grant Congress the power to make national immigration laws). But it was in the far more progressive dissent to a different 1890s decision that the Court most explicitly reflected these exclusionary attitudes toward Chinese Americans. In the course of his famous dissent to the *Plessy v. Ferguson* (1896) decision and its legal support for racial segregation, Justice John

Marshall Harlan overtly contrasted African Americans (for whose civils rights and "equality under the law" he was passionately arguing) with Chinese Americans, calling the latter "a race so different from our own that we do not permit those belonging to it to become citizens of the United States." Two years later, Harlan would reiterate these sentiments in a public lecture, arguing of Chinese Americans that "this is a race utterly foreign to us and never will assimilate with us." That xenophobic and exclusionary sentiment toward Chinese Americans underlay the Yellow Peril narrative, the period's mob movements and violence, and the development of immigration laws designed overtly to force Chinese Americans out of the United States.

Despite those exclusionary efforts, Chinese Americans remained a present and prominent American community throughout the late nineteenth century. There were more than 104,000 Chinese Americans listed on the 1880 Census and more than 106,000 on the 1890 Census, an impressive stability given the decade's numerous attempts to limit and destroy that community. Of course the xenophobic narratives and political campaigns, the mob violence, and exclusionary laws had their effects, and the story of Chinese American lives, families, and communities from 1880 through at least World War II (and in many ways through the 1965 Immigration Act) is one of partial resistance and perseverance in the face of these constant forces and threats. But a series of late-nineteenth- and early-twentieth-century inspiring figures and triumphs help us better remember an alternative, inclusive vision of Chinese American history and community, one in which these stories exemplify American ideals both in response to and beyond such dark histories.

One of those figures, Wong Kim Ark, was the subject of his own, far more inclusive and inspiring, 1890s Supreme Court case and decision. Wong was born in San Francisco sometime around 1870 to two Chinese immigrant parents, referred to in documents as Wong Si Ping and Wee Lee; as my phrases there suggest, even the basic details of Wong's early life and heritage are ambiguous, due in large part to the challenges of life in America for all Chinese Americans in this period (Wong's parents, for example, were never able to gain American citizenship despite apparently living in the nation for many decades). What's more definite is that Wong was working as a cook in San Francisco in November 1894, when he sailed to China for a visit with family there. When he attempted to return to the United States in August 1895, the Port of San Francisco's Collector of Customs denied him entry, arguing that despite his birth in the United States, Wong was not an American citizen because of his Chinese parents and thus under the Scott Act he was not legally able to leave the United States and return. Another post–Exclusion Act provision gave customs officers absolute and unquestioned authority to apply these exclusionary laws as they saw fit, and Wong was thus detained on ships off the California coast for five months at the behest of the collector of customs.

San Francisco's Chinatown and Chinese American community were among the many on the West Coast that long predated Anglo and U.S. arrival to California, and Wong benefitted directly from that longstanding and deeply rooted cultural community. More specifically, he received the aid of the city's Chinese Consolidated Benevolent Association (CCBA), a combination and more officially incorporated descendent of the so-called Six Companies that had in many ways run Chinatown in the early part of the nineteenth century. The Companies were often described by outsiders as criminal enterprises, perceptions no doubt influenced by the Yellow Peril narratives of the era, but seem to have functioned much more as neighborhood associations; the city's Chinese American community did also feature separate "fighting tongs" that were more directly linked to criminal activities such as opium and gambling. In any case, by the 1890s the CCBA had emerged as an entirely reputable and progressive force in Chinatown and San Francisco society. With the financial and legal support of the CCBA, Wong and his allies filed a writ of habeas corpus in federal district court, challenging his detention and arguing for his citizenship as a natural-born American.

Wong's situation and case fell complicatedly between a pair of national legal documents: the Fourteenth Amendment, which cemented the concept of "birthright citizenship" (the idea that anyone born in the United States and not the child of foreign government employees was a U.S. citizen by birth); and the 1870 Naturalization Act, which had sought to separate Chinese and Asian Americans from such shared concepts of citizenship. In the years between the 1870 Act and Wong's case, a number of circuit court cases had addressed the question of whether American-born Chinese Americans were U.S. citizens, with each ruling determining that they were; the most well-known, California's *In re Look Tin Sing* (1884), featured a similar case to Wong's, of a California-born Chinese American who was barred from reentering the U.S. after a trip to China and whose U.S. citizenship the California federal circuit court upheld. But the Supreme Court had not had the opportunity to rule on such a case, and might not have in Wong's case either if not for exclusionary attitudes: San Francisco attorney George Collins, who had published an article in the May/June 1895 issue of the *American Law Review* criticizing the *Look Tin Sing* ruling and arguing that Chinese Americans had no right to citizenship, was seeking a test case to bring before the Supreme Court; he convinced a like-minded U.S. attorney, Henry Foote, to pursue Wong's case in order to cement that anti-Chinese perspective in federal law.

Wong's case first went before California district judge William Morrow in late 1895, with Wong's attorneys citing *Look Tin Sing* and other cases as direct precedent; Morrow agreed, and on January 3, 1896, declared Wong a U.S. citizen due to his native birth. Collins, Foote, and their exclusionary official allies immediately appealed the decision to the Supreme Court, with the U.S. solicitor general Holmes Conrad arguing on the government's behalf that Wong and other native-born Chinese Americans were not eligible for citizenship. Not surprisingly, Justice John Harlan sided with the government, and he was joined by Chief Justice Melville Fuller, arguing that "the children of Chinese born in this country do not, *ipso facto*, become citizens of the United States unless the fourteenth amendment overrides both treaty and statute." But they were the only two dissenters in the Court's March 1898, 6–2 decision in favor of Wong; in that decision, written by Justice Horace Gray, the majority noted that "during all the time of their said residence in the United States, as domiciled residents therein, the said mother and father of said Wong Kim Ark were engaged in the prosecution of business, and were never engaged in any diplomatic or official capacity under the emperor of China." Since he was not subject to such an exception, the Court ruled, Wong Kim Ark was indeed a U.S. citizen.

Despite the somewhat specific and narrow elements of that decision, the impact of Wong's case was much more far-reaching and sweeping than that. An exclusionary March 30, 1898, editorial in the *San Francisco Chronicle* recognized those possibilities, worrying that the ruling "may have a wider effect upon the question of citizenship than the public supposes," and adding that "it may become necessary . . . to amend the Federal Constitution and definitely limit citizenship to whites and blacks." The Constitution was never so amended, however, and instead *United States v. Wong Kim Ark* helped cement the Fourteenth Amendment's concept of birthright citizenship and make clear that it, and thus the protections and rights of the United States Constitution itself, extended to virtually all Americans (Native Americans were still overtly excluded and would remain so until the 1924 Indian Citizenship Act). While the Supreme Court of course played a crucial role in that arc, it was a young San Francisco cook and his allies in the city's longstanding Chinatown community who really launched the efforts that led to that hugely significant legal, philosophical, and national progress.

Influential and inspiring as that progress was, however, Wong, like Look Tin Sing and the subjects of the other parallel late-nineteenth-century court cases, was born in the United States. For Chinese immigrants to America, the group most overtly and fully targeted by the Yellow Peril narrative and the Chinese Exclusion Act and the period's other attacks (literal as well as figurative), the situation was even more fragile and fraught, and the exclusionary attitudes even stronger and more destructive. Developing an inclusive narrative of American history and identity that can feature such immigrant arrivals just as centrally as native-born Chinese Americans represents a significant step further still, and one with potential effects even more sweeping and salient to our own moment. And we have an impressive individual starting point and model for that inclusive narrative in one of the nineteenth century's most unique and exemplary Americans, Yung Wing (1828–1912).

Yung came to the United States in 1847, at the age of nineteen, and by that time had already experienced a number of cross-cultural educational and communal spaces. As he narrates those early experiences in his autobiography, *My Life in China and America* (1909, and our main source of information for much of Yung's early life and identity in particular), at the early age of seven years old, Yung was put into the missionary school of Mrs. Gutzlaff, the wife of an English missionary who had come to the city of Macao (not far from Yung's home village of Nam Ping). Although Yung admits to being unclear why his parents placed him (and not his older brother) into such a school, he imagines that the goals were overtly cross-cultural, writing, "I can only account for the departure thus taken on the theory that as foreign intercourse with China was just beginning to grow, my parents, anticipating that it might soon assume the proportions of a tidal wave, thought it worthwhile to take time by the forelock and put one of their sons to learning English that he might become one of the advanced interpreters and have a more advantageous position from which to make his way into the business and diplomatic world." And indeed Yung's time at Gutzlaff's school led him to subsequent, more advanced cross-cultural educational settings in China and, through them, to the American missionaries with whom he and two other young Chinese men would travel to the United States in early 1847.

Over the next few years, Yung would continue his cross-cultural educational and social experiences, attending Monson Academy (a preparatory high school) in Massachusetts and becoming acclimated to New England and the United States. By the time of his 1850 graduation from Monson, his two fellow arrivals had left, and Yung alone remained to pursue his Chinese American educational and professional goals and futures. His desired next step was to attend Yale College, but his missionary supporters would only help pay for that opportunity if Yung promised to return to China after college to continue their religious mission. Since Yung believed that "the calling of a missionary is not the only sphere of life where one can do the most good in China or elsewhere," he graciously declined their offer, finding others ways to fund his college education (including both the support of friends he had made in the U.S. and working various jobs during his time at Yale). This early turning point in Yung's Chinese American experiences not only allowed him to fulfill his next cross-cultural and educational goals (gaining U.S. citizenship in 1852 and becoming in 1854 the first Chinese American graduate of an American college) but also pushed him to think more deeply about his future goals. As he concludes the Yale chapter of his autobiography, "Before the close of my last year in college I had already sketched out what I should do. I was determined that the rising generation of

China should enjoy the same educational advantages that I had enjoyed. . . . To accomplish that object became the guiding star of my ambition."

It would be nearly twenty years before Yung succeeded in creating that cross-cultural educational opportunity, and along the way, while working as a diplomat between the two nations, he would experience a number of other turning points that exemplified his inspiring, inclusive Chinese American identity. In 1864, while on a diplomatic mission to secure industrial and military machinery for the Chinese government from a company in Fitchburg (Massachusetts), Yung attended a college reunion and then, perhaps inspired in part by that communal experience, decided to travel to Washington, DC, and volunteer for the Union Army. As he told the volunteer department's director, Brigadier-General James Barnes (himself the father of a Yale class-mate of Yung's, William Barnes), Yung was "anxious to offer my ser-vices . . . as an evidence of my loyalty and patriotism to my adopted coun-try." Indeed, he adds in the autobiography's account of this moment, "as a naturalized citizen of the United States, it was my bounden duty to" volun-teer. Barnes was "quite interested and pleased" but turned down Yung's offer; Yung was disappointed but "felt that I had at least fulfilled my duty to my adopted country." Indeed, he had, and during one of the Civil War's most destructive periods, certainly a moment that reflects Yung's evolving and exemplary Chinese American identity.

Yung experienced and contributed to three very different cross-cultural, Chinese American transformations in the 1870s. In 1873, while on a diplo-matic mission back to China, he encountered a Peruvian commissioner who was seeking to import additional forced Chinese laborers into his nation; these involuntary workers, known in the language of the period as "coolies," experienced a far more fraught and painful version of immigration and the Americas than had Yung. Although the commissioner tried to convince Yung that the workers were well treated, Yung responded with his own knowledge of "the facts and horrors of the coolie traffic," and then went further still: convincing the Chinese viceroy to investigate the trade's realities in both Peru and Cuba (two of its principle sites), and himself taking on the role of investigating the Peruvian situation. Yung worked diligently in this investi-gative role on behalf of his Chinese American brethren, compiling not only a written report but also accompanying photographs of the workers' wounds and scars, "taken in the night, unknown to anyone but the victims them-selves." Thanks to the efforts of Yung and his fellow investigator Chin Lan Pin, the viceroy cut off all ties with these nations and "the traffic received its death blow," a reflection of Yung's desire and willingness to change the experiences of Chinese Americans and communities far beyond his own.

Two years later, Yung achieved a far more personal but just as inspiring cross-cultural milestone, marrying Mary Kellogg of Avon, Connecticut, in March 1875. He doesn't write at all about their courtship or marriage in his autobiography (likely out of a sense of privacy), and so relatively little is known of Mary or how their relationship began. But a March 2 *New York Times* notice on the wedding highlights its particularly cross-cultural nature: Mary "wore a dress of white crape, imported expressly for this occasion from China," while Yung, "who long since adopted our style, appeared in full evening dress"; and at the reception "Chinese delicacies were mingled with . . . dishes of American style." And Yung and Mary's marriage produced two embodiments of that cross-cultural relationship, their sons Morrison Brown Yung and Bartlett Golden Yung: each named after individuals and families who had been vital parts of Yung's immigration to and early experiences in America; and both in the course of their lives following in their father's Chinese American footsteps in multiple ways, including attendance at Yale and work as diplomats between the United States and China.

By the time of both Yung's Peru investigation and his wedding, he had also achieved his long-gestating goal to create a cross-cultural educational opportunity for other young Chinese men. The Chinese Educational Mission (CEM) opened in 1872 with a permanent headquarters in Hartford, Connecticut (so as to have "the educational mission as deeply rooted in the United States as possible," Yung writes in this chapter of his autobiography), and a plan to bring 120 Chinese young men to follow directly the model of Yung's Chinese American experiences: attending preparatory schools and colleges throughout New England; continuing to study both Chinese language and culture and English and American history (among other cross-cultural topics); the opportunity for advanced students to enlist in the Military Academy at West Point or Naval Academy at Annapolis (an experience guaranteed not only by the CEM charter but by the 1868 Burlingame Treaty between the United States and China); and, overall, "the gradual but marked transformation of the students in their behavior and conduct as they grew in knowledge and stature under New England influence." Those Chinese American transformations were perhaps the CEM's most overarching goal, and thus it gave Yung particular pleasure to remark that, not long after the students' arrival, "now in New England the heavy weight of repression and suppression was lifted from the minds of these young students," and "they exulted in their freedom and leaped for joy."

Those transformed, Chinese American identities took a number of forms for the CEM students, but one especially inclusive American example was the CEM's baseball team. Known officially as the Orientals but usually referred to by their preferred name, the Celestials, the team featured students who had been star athletes at Yale (among other college squads) and in the mid-1870s joined one of the era's new semipro baseball leagues, making quite a name for themselves on that regional circuit. William Lyon Phelps, a high school and Yale classmate of many of the CEM students and later a prominent literary scholar at Yale, would dedicate a chapter of his 1939

autobiography to his "Chinese Schoolmates," and highlights in particular
there the Celestials' athletic successes. Of "Tsang [probably Wu Yang-
zeng]," for example, Lyon notes that he "was a great pitcher, impossible to
hit." Another of the team's star pitchers, Liang Dunyan, seems to have been
nicknamed Lefty, such a stereotypical baseball detail (in the best possible
sense) that it needs no additional explanation. Indeed, the story of baseball
itself, like that of sports in America more broadly, is in many ways constructed out of such iconic details and identities, and the connection of the
CEM team and students to some of the earliest such iconic baseball stories
reflects just how much the members of this Chinese American community
(like its exemplary and inspiring founder) were becoming an integral part of
their America throughout the 1870s.

That 1870s America was also moving inexorably toward the Exclusion Act,
however, and those xenophobic and exclusionary trends had tragic effects on
both the Educational Mission and Yung's own life and family. When the first
group of CEM students applied for admission to the military academies in
1878, they were summarily denied, in violation of both the CEM charter and
the Burlingame Treaty. As Yung describes the moment in his autobiography,
tying it directly to both those exclusionary historical trends and their eventual
legal outcomes, "The answer to my application was: 'There is no room
provided for Chinese students.' It was curt and disdainful. It breathed the
spirit of Kearneyism and Sandlotism with which the whole Pacific atmosphere was impregnated, and which had hypnotized all the departments of the
government, especially Congress. . . . The race prejudice against the Chinese
was so rampant and rank, . . . that the Burlingame Treaty of 1868 was,
without the least provocation . . . trampled under foot unceremoniously and
wantonly, and set aside as though no such treaty had ever existed, in order to
make way for those acts of congressional discrimination against Chinese
immigration which were pressed for immediate enactment." Enraged by this
American abandonment of the CEM, the Chinese government withdrew its
own support, and by 1881 the school was closed and the majority of the
students were forced to leave the United States.

The school's closure was but the first of what Yung would call a series of
"blows that fell upon me one after the other . . . [and] were enough to crush
my spirit." He was called back to China to deal with the aftermath of these
events, and while he was abroad, Mary heard rumors that he might be executed; "this piece of gratuitous information tended more to aggravate a mind
already weighed down by poor health," and Mary grew progressively worse
and passed away in June 1886, leaving behind nine- and seven-year-old sons.
With the help of his mother-in-law, Yung did all he could to become "both
father and mother" to the boys, his "whole soul wrapped up in their education
and well-being," but the exclusion era had not finished with Yung yet. In

1896, he was ordered back to China once more, and this time when he sought to return to the United States he was not allowed back in; his U.S. citizenship had been stripped by the Chinese Exclusion Act, and although Secretary of State John Sherman admitted (in an April 1898 letter to the diplomat corresponding with Yung) that "a refusal to admit now his right to privileges which he has apparently exercised for many years would on its face seem unjust and without warrant. Nevertheless, in view of the construction placed upon the naturalization laws of the United States by our highest courts, the Department does not feel that it can properly recognize him as a citizen of the United States." Yung was legally barred from returning to the U.S. and his home in Hartford, and officially was only present in America one more time, for his younger son Bartlett's 1902 graduation from Yale.

That was Yung's only official visit to the United States over the final fifteen years of his life. However, I believe that he spent a good deal more time here than that, as an inspiring, inclusive example of a very early "illegal immigrant." Yung ends his autobiography in 1902, but signs the book's preface, "November, 1909, 15 Atwood St., Hartford, Conn.," perhaps a reflection on where he has spent much of those subsequent seven years. Similarly, his April 22, 1912, *New York Times* obituary, submitted to the paper from Hartford, notes that Yung "died at his home here today, in his eighty-fourth year," and amidst the details of his life story remarks simply, "in 1902 he came back to America." Of course Yung's connections to China remained part of that story to the end as well, and both sides of that Chinese American identity are reflected in the obituary's reference to his children: "He leaves two sons, Morrison, of Hartford, and Bartlett, who is now at Shanghai." Clearly this next generation of the Yung family would carry on his (and Mary's) cross-cultural, inclusive Chinese American identity, one that, exclusionary attitudes and laws notwithstanding, seems clearly to have continued to unfold in the United States over the final years of Yung's inspiring life.

The CEM students represented another side to that next generation, of course, and there too we find inclusive alternatives to the exclusion era and its effects on the school. (The descendants of the CEM students have created a website, CEM Connections, that traces the lives and legacies of all 120 students quite thoroughly.) Even those students who did return to China brought their CEM experiences and cross-cultural identities back with them in compelling and influential ways: exemplifying that legacy is Jeme Tien Yau, a former member of the Celestials baseball team who subsequently graduated from Yale in 1881 with a degree in civil engineering, returned permanently to China in that same year, and became over the next few decades one of that nation's most prominent and productive civil and naval engineers. In 1908, Jeme's two sons were able to transcend the limitations of the exclusion era, travel to the United States, and enter college there, one studying mechanical engineering at New York's Tri-State College and the other following in Jeme's footsteps to study civil engineering at Yale. This multigenerational and multinational Chinese American story, one that unfolded in the depths of the exclusion era, was not at all atypical of the CEM students.

Some students did find ways to stay in the United States, though, and their stories reflect with particular force the Chinese American community's resistance to and perseverance through the exclusion era. Exemplifying that community is Chang Hon Yen, a graduate of first Yale and then Columbia Law School who fought not only to stay in America but for the right to practice law here. Initially denied admission to the New York bar due to his race, Chang, with the aid of legal allies, lobbied the state legislature to pass a bill (written by Chang himself) that granted him an exception and access to the bar. He then traveled to San Francisco and for many years worked on behalf of both the existing Chinese American community there and those arrivals affected by the Exclusion Act and detained on ships in San Francisco Harbor, all despite being denied full legal standing by the California Supreme Court due to his status as a "Mongolian." Chang would go on to serve in multiple legal and governmental roles across the late-nineteenth and early-twentieth centuries, greatly affecting his adopted nation in inclusive ways that challenge and transcend any exclusionary attempt to define him as outside of or foreign to its community.

Before they were forced to disband in the aftermath of the CEM's closure, the Celestials baseball team experienced a final, symbolic moment that likewise modeled that inclusive Chinese American identity. Most of the players were among the majority of the students who traveled to San Francisco in the summer of 1881, to take a steamship away from their adopted home and back to China. While they awaited that departure, a local Oakland baseball team challenged the Celestials to a game. It's unclear whether that challenge represented bad or good sportsmanship, one final twist of the exclusionary screw or a brief respite from such divisions and discriminations; in any case, student Wen Bing Chung would later write, "the Oakland men imagined that they were going to have a walk-over with the Chinese," but the Celestials rose to this almost unimaginable moment and won their final game by a score of 11–8, per a September 4, 1881, story in the *San Francisco Chronicle*. The next day they boarded their steamer—but whether they left the U.S. permanently like Jeme, left but subsequently (if illegally) returned like Yung, or found ways to stay like Chang, all of those in the CEM community, like this symbolic final baseball victory, illustrated the vital Chinese American presence in and contribution to a multilayered, inclusive American community.

Appearing in print a few decades after the Celestials' final game, two short pieces by Sui Sin Far (1865–1914), one of the first Chinese American authors to publish journalism and fiction in English, offer one more way to

consider both the exclusionary and inclusive sides to Chinese American identities and communities in this era. Far was born Edith Maude Eaton in Mac-
clesfield, England, daughter of an English merchant father and a Chinese
mother who had been adopted by English missionaries; the family moved to
Montreal when she was a young girl. Eaton began publishing journalistic
pieces in the city's English-language newspapers (the *Montreal Star* and the
Daily Witness) when she was still a teenager, using the pseudonym Sui Sin
Far (the Cantonese name of the popular narcissus flower). In young adult-
hood she moved briefly to Kingston, Jamaica, and then to San Francisco; she
would spend most of the rest of her life in the United States (including
extended stints in both Seattle and Boston), working as a legal secretary and
freelance journalist while gradually assembling the collection of interconnected short stories that she would eventually publish in book form as *Mrs.
Spring Fragrance and Tales of Chinese Children* (1912).

One of those short stories, "In the Land of the Free" (originally published
in *The Independent* magazine in September 1909), reflects some of the darkest realities and effects (and ironies, as her bitingly sarcastic title suggests) of
the exclusion era on Chinese American families and communities. Far's
story opens with one of her protagonists, Lae Choo, returning to San Francisco after a trip to China to care for her husband Hom Hing's dying mother;
while in China Lae Choo has given birth to the couple's first child, an infant
son who is meeting his father for the first time there at the dock. But the
family also meets U.S. customs officers there and, because of various
post–Exclusion Act laws and policies (such as the Scott Act's restrictions on
Chinese Americans leaving the United States and returning and the Geary
Act's requirement that all Chinese Americans carry residency papers at all
times or risk deportation), those officers take the despondent couple's young
son away from them. "Thus," Far ends the story's first section (of four), "was
the law of the land complied with."

Much of the remainder of Far's brief story is set in the couple's Chinatown apartment, where we follow their consistently frustrated attempts to get
their child back, partially aided but also abused by a young white lawyer
whose promised ability to navigate the era's discriminatory laws and bureau-
cracies allows him to take most of the couple's money. Finally, ten months
after the family separation, Lae Choo is able to reunite with her son in the
"mission nursery school" where he has been detained—but it is perhaps too
late, as the young child, now "dressed in blue cotton overalls and white-soled
shoes," shrinks away from Lae Choo and her "hungry arms," "trie[s] to hide
himself in the folds of the white woman's skirt," and tells his mother
"Go'way, go'way!" While this Chinese American family has not been literally excluded from the United States, the nation's exclusionary laws and attitudes have quite possibly destroyed, and certainly forever altered, their little,
loving American community.

In the same year and the same magazine, Far also published one of her most autobiographical journalistic pieces, "Leaves from the Mental Portfolio of an Eurasian." Using anecdotes from across the many stages and settings of her cross-cultural, English-Chinese-Canadian-American life, Far's piece traces the fraught and fragile but also consistent and inspiring development of her identity and perspective. She certainly does not shy away from xenophobic and exclusionary moments and attitudes, from children who chant "Chinky, Chinaman, yellow-face, pig-tail, rat-eater" at Far and her brother during a childhood trip across the border to Hudson, New York, to an American employer who, not knowing his legal secretary's multiracial heritage (she was apparently able to pass for European American), notes that "I cannot reconcile myself to the thought that the Chinese are human." In that latter moment, Far stands up for her community and culture, responding, "The Chinese people may have no souls, no expression on their faces, be altogether beyond the pale of civilization, but whatever they are, I want you to understand that I am—I am a Chinese."

Despite such exclusionary moments, I would argue that the whole of Far's piece, like indeed the whole of her writing career, comprises an inclusive attempt to represent both that Chinese American community and her own goals and role as a literary ambassador between that community and its nation. Elsewhere in the piece she highlights with "joy" the response of a New York Chinese American to her journalistic efforts: "The Chinese in America," he argued in a letter to a New York paper, "owe an everlasting debt of gratitude to Sui Sin Far for the bold stand she has taken in their defense." And she ends the piece with a number of inspiring images of both her multiple communities and her own cross-cultural identity: "My experiences as an Eurasian never cease; but people are not now as prejudiced as they have been"; "So I roam backward and forward across the continent. When I am East, my heart is West. When I am West, my heart is East. Before long I hope to be in China"; "I give my right hand to the Occidentals and my left to the Orientals, hoping that between them they will not utterly destroy the insignificant 'connecting link.' And that's all."

All that Sui Sin Far offered in her writing, that Yung Wing and the Chinese Educational Mission students offered as a model community, that Wong Kim Ark offered as a legal argument for citizenship, was and remains far from insignificant. Each on their own terms, and even more so collectively, these figures and stories, voices and histories offer a potent, inclusive challenge to the era's exclusionary narratives and laws, an alternative vision of Chinese Americans as exemplary members of an American community and identity.

Chapter Six

Fears and Facts of Filipino America

The late-nineteenth and early-twentieth-century U.S. occupation of the Philippines produced exclusionary attitudes and discrimination toward Filipino Americans on a number of interconnected levels. That occupation began as an important early military campaign during the 1898 Spanish American War: President McKinley signed a joint congressional resolution declaring war on Spain on April 20, 1898; and on May 1, Commodore George Dewey's naval armada engaged with Spanish forces in Manila Bay. Over the next few months, U.S. and Spanish forces would fight for control of the islands, while the United States also successfully fended off aggressive attempts by multiple other European nations, particularly Germany, to stake their claim to this suddenly up-for-grabs and prized Pacific island chain. The Spanish commanding general, Fermin Jaudenes, surrendered the islands to U.S. forces on August 14, and the terms of the December 10 Treaty of Paris that formally ended the Spanish American War included the ceding of the Philippines (along with Puerto Rico and Guam, and in a more temporary way, Cuba) over to the United States.

The question of whether the Philippines would remain under U.S. control after the war was initially an open and contested one. During the war, Commodore Dewey had enlisted the aid of Emilio Aguinaldo, the leader of an 1898 Filipino rebellion against the Spanish who had been living in exile in Hong Kong. Aguinaldo helped rally Filipino forces to fight against the Spanish and also declared the Philippines independent as early as June 12 (although the United States did not recognize that declaration). While Aguinaldo envisioned an entirely independent nation with himself as leader—he and his allies declared himself president of the Philippines on January 1, 1899, just a few weeks after the Treaty of Paris—the United States began to develop other plans for the islands. On January 20, President McKinley estab-

lished the First Philippine Commission (or Schurman Commission) to study
the question of Filipino sovereignty; given that one of the commission's five
members was Commodore Dewey himself, and another the islands' military
governor Elwell Otis, it is perhaps not a surprise that the commission concluded, in its January 3, 1900, final report that "the United States cannot
withdraw.... The Filipinos are wholly unprepared for independence."

Aguinaldo and millions of Filipinos disagreed, and did so consistently
and forcefully: nearly a year before the Schurman Commission filed that
report, and for many years after, Filipino rebels engaged in a violent conflict
with the occupying U.S. troops for control of the islands. That Philippine
American War, or Philippine Insurrection as it was generally known in the
United States, began with the Second Battle of Manila in February 1899, as
forces of President Aguinaldo's First Philippine Republic sought to expel
U.S. troops from the city. The war would stretch for more than three bloody
years, officially ending with the capture of Aguinaldo in July 1902; sporadic
further resistance, led by General Macario Sakay and the rebel government
known as the Tagalog Republic, continued for more than a decade after that
point. At least 200,000 Filipinos died in the course of the conflict, with many
millions more displaced and affected.

As is so often the case with military conflicts, the Philippine American
War produced a great deal of anti-Filipino propaganda in the United States.
Those efforts began as early as a front-page political cartoon in the *Boston
Sunday Globe* of March 5, 1899; the cartoon, entitled "Expansion, Before
and After," used both familiar American images of blackface minstrelsy and
depictions of Filipinos as unclothed savages to create a multilayered, racist
and xenophobic portrayal of this uncivilized other. Although a few prominent American writers and cultural figures, calling themselves the Anti-Imperialist League, resisted such propaganda and criticized the U.S. imperial
presence in the Philippines—most famously Mark Twain, whose anti-imperi-
al essay, "To the Person Sitting in Darkness," appeared in the *North
American Review* in February 1901—for the great majority of Americans
these racist, hostile images were their consistent source of information about
both the Philippine American War and Filipinos through these turn-of-the-
century years.

Those burgeoning anti-Filipino narratives in the United States would become particularly significant and ironic over the next few decades. A striking
effect of both the war and its displacements and the ongoing U.S. occupation
of the Philippines (through which the islands became a U.S. protectorate and
their inhabitants part of the expanding American empire) was that tens of
thousands of Filipinos immigrated to the United States in the first decades of
the twentieth century. Some did so in the special category of *pensionados*,
young men invited to study on scholarship at American universities (in what
would become the largest American scholarship program prior to the estab-

lishment of the Fulbright in 1948), but most did so as migrant laborers, generally arriving on the West Coast and working throughout California and the Pacific Northwest. While these immigrants, in what came to be known as the manong generation, were as I discuss below far from the first Filipino Americans, they did comprise the largest and most widespread community of Filipino arrivals in U.S. history. Moreover, because of the islands' protected status, the era's expanding exclusions of other Asian immigrants (such as the 1917 Immigration Act, which created an "Asiatic Barred Zone") did not affect Filipino arrivals nor restrict this wave of immigration.

That wave of new Filipino immigrants arrived to a society in which the wartime xenophobic propaganda had been simmering for years; as these new arrivals became a more visible part of communities across the western United States, that xenophobia turned to exclusionary attitudes directed at Filipino Americans. By the 1920s, Filipino Americans had become a sizeable part of the labor force in many western communities, and the exclusionary attitudes evolved into overt, white supremacist hatred and violence (often fueled by the decade's resurgent Ku Klux Klan). Anti-Filipino riots and massacres occurred in the Yakima Valley in Washington in November 1927, the Wenatchee Valley in the same state in early 1928, and the city of Exeter in California's San Joaquin Valley in October 1929. The stock market crashed in the same week as the Exeter riot, and the Great Depression that followed only deepened these anti-Filipino sentiments. In January 1930, highly publicized romantic relationships between Filipino laborers and white women in Watsonville, California, served as the excuse upon which a rampaging white mob blamed their five-day destruction of the city's Filipino community, including the destruction of numerous businesses and homes and the assaults on and lynching of a number of Filipinos. That violence would spread throughout California, including the bombing of a Filipino club in Stockton and threats of lynchings directed at Filipino workers across the state.

The romantic and sexual fears that helped launch the Watsonville massacre were more than just a pretense; they also reflected another side of these exclusionary narratives, a desire to keep Filipino Americans from "mixing" with European American communities. California had had existing antimiscegenation laws on the books since at least 1880, but since Section 60 of the California Civil Code specifically forbid the marriage of white Americans to "negros," "mulattos," and "Mongolians" (generally accepted in the era to mean Chinese Americans), it was unclear whether Filipinos would be subject to these laws. In 1926 California attorney general Ulysses Webb argued in a public memo that Filipinos were indeed "Mongolian," and many counties across the state refused to grant marriage licenses to mixed-race couples featuring Filipino partners; but a series of early 1930s court decisions sided instead with such couples. When the California Supreme Court upheld one of those decisions, 1933's *Roldan v. Los Angeles County*, the State Legislature immediately amended Section 60, adding "members of the Malay race" to the list of those cultures that were legally barred from racial intermarriage with white partners.

While many of these bigoted and exclusionary riots and laws took place in the particular western states that featured the majority of the era's new Filipino arrivals, the nation as a whole likewise embraced anti-Filipino exclusion in the 1930s. It did so in particular through two national laws that, under the guise of support for the Philippines, sought both to limit future Filipino immigration and to destroy the existing Filipino American community. The Tydings-McDuffie Act (1934), also known as the Philippine Independence Act, established a new Commonwealth of the Philippines that would in ten years' time become a fully independent nation. While those steps were certainly significant and allowed the nation to elect its first democratically chosen president, Manuel Quezon, the law's most salient American purposes were revealed in two striking shifts: the establishment of a quota of fifty Filipino immigrants to the United States per year (a number so tiny as to be an exclusion act by another name), and the change in legal designation for not only these future arrivals but also and most stunningly all current Filipino Americans, from U.S. nationals to foreign aliens.

The following year, the 1935 Filipino Repatriation Act made the desired, exclusionary endpoint of these legal changes clearer still. Again, the law had a superficially supportive intent, as it provided funding for one-way transportation for all Filipino Americans wishing to return to the Philippines (or travel there for the first time, since, of course, by 1935 many members of even these new communities had been born in the United States). The alien status and miniscule immigration quota would still apply to any Filipino American who left, making clear that the trip would indeed almost certainly be a one-way journey. Making the law's intent even clearer was the testimony of California health official Edythe Tate Thompson, one of the nation's preeminent anti-Filipino voices and one of the most vocal advocates for both Tydings-McDuffie and (especially) the Repatriation Act. Although she publicly called for "voluntary deportation" of Filipino Americans, in a resolution submitted to the national commissioner of immigration she went further, requesting "that it be stipulated that Army transports be used to return these unfortunate dependent people to their own country at the earliest possible moment." She even noted that "perhaps a recommendation from him to the War Department might make it possible to use these transports without legislation," but Congress went along with such bigoted voices, passing these two discriminatory laws and cementing early-twentieth-century anti-Filipino exclusions as a national trend.

The problem with these exclusionary attitudes and laws isn't just that they were based entirely on xenophobia and prejudice, nor even that they flew in the face of the Philippines' status as a U.S. protectorate during this era (although both things were true and are important to remember). These anti-Filipino exclusions were also profoundly inaccurate to the history of this culture and community in America. The early twentieth century did see the largest waves of Filipino arrivals, and they did tend to immigrate to West Coast areas where there had not been noticeable Filipino American communities prior to this period. But at the same time, the Filipino American community comprised one of the oldest and most deeply rooted Asian American communities, having been a part of America for more than a century by the time of the U.S. occupation of the islands.

According to Filipino American oral history and folklore, the first Filipino arrivals were fishermen and sailors who disembarked from Spanish ships and began to settle the Barataria Bay region, on the gulf coast of Spanish Louisiana, around 1765. Much of Louisiana had been ceded to Spain by France a few years earlier, as part of the Treaty of Fontainebleu (1762) that helped conclude the French and Indian War, and the Spanish had immediately begun to extend their New Spain colonial presence into the region. The Philippines had been a territory of the viceroy of New Spain for two centuries by that time, and both Filipino sailors and ships (known as Manila galleons, the largest wooden ships ever built) formed an important part of the Spanish nautical and colonial enterprise. It is virtually certain that Filipinos would thus have been part of Spain's explorations and settlements of Louisiana after the region became part of New Spain, and according to these folk histories some of those Filipino sailors decided to remain in the area, establishing fishing villages (primarily one known as St. Malo) around Barataria Bay in the last few decades of the eighteenth century.

It's important to note that historians have not been able to find primary sources documenting these eighteenth-century arrivals; the first Filipino American communities for which we have such documentation are from the turn of the nineteenth century, as I will discuss in a moment. Given the newly established nature of Spain's presence in Louisiana at all, and moreover given that these Filipino villages were by all accounts established outside of official Spanish policy, it stands to reason that there would not be much formal documentation of their origins or initial existence. Indeed, the very absence of primary source documentation could instead highlight just how foundational and longstanding these villages were as part of the region's postcontact history and identity. And finally, while the precise details of the villages' establishment might never be known, their presence in Filipino American folk and collective oral history itself suggests the significance of these origin points for a community, one that can thus trace its roots back into some of the earliest moments of colonial Louisiana and America.

In any case, by the turn of the nineteenth century a few decades later, the Filipino American presence in Southern Louisiana was a clearly established one. That region of Louisiana had become a particularly diverse area, first during the decades of Spanish rule (when immigrants from Spain, arrivals from elsewhere in New Spain like the Philippines, and Isleños from the Canary Islands had all formed their own fishing villages in the area) and continuing after Napoleon purchased Louisiana back for France in 1800. When the United States purchased "Louisiana" (in this case an area including a wide swath of territory across the continent, although New Orleans and coastal Louisiana were Thomas Jefferson's first priority in the deal) from France three years later, these multicultural southern Louisiana villages became part of the expanding United States, and their existence and inhabitants were also documented in English for the first time.

The earliest such documented Filipino arrival seems to have been discovered by the influential Filipino American historian Sixto Lopez. Lopez, who initially came to the United States in 1898 as part of a Filipino delegation during the Spanish American War and would return for a much longer sojourn in 1900 (partly to advocate for Filipino independence and self-rule), published an article on early Filipino American settlers in the December 6, 1903, issue of the *Springfield (MA) Republican*. There Lopez highlights "one Augustin Felicano, a Bicol, from the island of Catanduanes, southeast of Luzon, who, after having fought in the battle of Trafalgar as a petty officer on one of the Spanish ships of the line, retired from the navy of the Peninsula and set sail for New Orleans in 1807." Interestingly, these nautical origin points for Felicano's Filipino American journey parallel the folk histories of how St. Malo and other Baratarian villages were initially settled, and highlight how much the multinational colonial history of Louisiana continued to influence its evolving multicultural identity and community even after the region became part of the United States.

Over the next few years, as Sixto puts it, "the Manila-men gradually increased," and this blossoming Filipino American community would find themselves complicatedly but centrally part of a foundational American history: the War of 1812's Battle of New Orleans. That battle's very existence is a complicated one, since most of it was fought after the British had already ratified the Treaty of Ghent that effectively ended the war: the British ratified on December 27, 1814, but the treaty did not reach Washington for U.S. ratification until February 17; and in between those dates most of the war's culminating battle, the Battle of New Orleans, would take place. Whatever its official significance, of course, the battle was very real for all those who fought in it—and on the U.S. side, the military forces comprised one of the most diverse armies in American history. Although the U.S. commanding general was Andrew Jackson, one of the most overt white supremacists in U.S. military history (soon to receive his reputation as an "Indian killer" in multiple bloody conflicts with Southeastern tribes), the troops who fought in his army at New Orleans included Native Americans from a number of

Louisiana tribes, African Americans from the city's "free men of color" community, and, most complicatedly still and most relevantly for this chapter, "Baratarians" under the command of the French Creole pirate Jean Lafitte.

The participation of Lafitte and his Baratarian forces (which included a number of Filipino Americans, generally referred to in historical accounts as Manila-men) in the Battle of New Orleans was not entirely voluntary. The Caribbean-born Lafitte and his brother Pierre had been operating smuggling and piracy operations out of New Orleans for some time; after the passage of the U.S. Embargo Act of 1807, which cracked down on such illicit activities in major ports, they moved their base of operations to the Barataria Bay region. In September 1814, as a complement to their War of 1812 military operations, U.S. naval forces invaded the area and captured most of Lafitte's fleet; they would subsequently grant Lafitte and his men provisional pardons in exchange for their service during the Battle of New Orleans. Yet I would argue that this complicated origin for Filipino American military service fits well within the long history of the American military, which alongside volunteers and career soldiers has of course consistently included various forms of involuntary drafts, mercenaries and other compensated soldiers, and soldiers who fight in order to avoid prison or other less desirable alternatives. Many of the American soldiers in these latter categories have come from immigrant and other minority communities, and, whatever the origins of their service, most have gone on to fight with courage and distinction alongside their comrades. By all accounts, the Manila-men did likewise in the Battle of New Orleans, and a number of contemporary drawings and reports captured the efforts of these Filipino American soldiers as they helped the fledgling United States secure its status as an independent nation in the Early Republic period.

These south Louisiana Filipino American communities continued to develop across the course of the nineteenth century, with a few particularly significant moments along the way. Sixto Lopez highlights another one tied to a national military conflict: the community's decision to side with the Union in the Civil War. As Lopez writes, "To their lasting credit be it said, they joined and fought with the soldiers of the Union in order to free the slave, and some of the blood that helped to wash the stain of slavery from 'Old Glory' was Filipino blood. A widow of one of these Filipinos still lives in New Orleans, and is the recipient of a small pension from the United States government." Nestor P. Enriguez, a twentieth-century Filipino immigrant who served in the U.S. Navy as a submarine chief petty officer and has since become a prominent amateur historian of Filipino Americans, has identified by name at least four of the particular Manila-men who joined the Union Navy during the Civil War: Caystana Baltazar, Andrew Belino, Antonio Ducasin, and Sabas

Pilisardo. Despite those small numbers, the act of joining the Union forces despite their location deep in Confederate Louisiana reflects the continued commitment of these Filipino Americans to the future and fate of their new nation.

Five years after the Civil War's end, members of this community took a significant step to ensure their own collective future. In 1870, residents of St. Malo studying in New Orleans founded la Socieded de Beneficencia de los Hispanos Filipinos, the first Filipino association in the United States. Like other neighborhood associations and community organizations, La Socieded helped welcome new arrivals and ensure their successful transition into the community, collected funds to aid community members in need and pre-served cultural legacies through such endeavors as a community vault where members' remains could be preserved. The association also worked to cele-brate both the community's heritage and its present national identity, orga-nizing Fourth of July celebrations but also, for example, commemorating José Rizal, the Filipino resistance leader who led an unsuccessful rebellion against the Spanish and was executed in December 1896. The creation and existence of La Sociedad reflected a Filipino American community truly putting down roots and becoming a more established and multigenerational American culture.

As it did so, the community also attracted national attention for the first time. Illustrating that new interest is "Saint Malo, a Lacustrine Village in Louisiana," a March 31, 1883, story for *Harper's Weekly*, one of the most widely read magazines of the era. Written by the prominent New Orleans local color author Lafcadio Hearn and featuring no less than ten illustrations, "Saint Malo" reads like a combination of travel writing, local color fiction, and an anthropological excursion to a distinctly unfamiliar world. Hearn's perspective is not without its prejudices, as when he writes of the village:

> its human inhabitants are not less strange, wild, picturesque. Most of them are cinnamon-colored men; a few are glossily yellow, like that bronze into which a small proportion of gold is worked by the molder. Their features are irregular without being actually repulsive; some have the cheek-bones very prominent and the eyes of several are set slightly aslant. . . . In Manila there are several varieties of the Malay race, and these Louisiana settlers represent more than one type.

As that last sentence reflects, Hearn's local color observations do extend beyond exotic stereotypes and into the specifics of this multifaceted American culture; to that end, toward the piece's conclusion he hears and transcribes carefully a song performed by the community's cantador as "the Manila men pass stormy evenings" in collective leisure and celebration.

By 1883, whenever we date the south Louisiana Filipino America com-munity's precise origins, this was indeed a multifaceted, multigenerational

American culture. They had seen three distinct national flags fly over the region, and had fought alongside fellow Americans against the forces of a fourth nation. They had lived in the South long enough to see it move from slavery to Civil War to Reconstruction and its aftermaths. They had participated in the region's fishing industry and trade for decades, becoming an integral part of the Gulf Coast economy in the process. As Hearn traces at length, they certainly had retained many of their specific and unique cultural elements, but of course so has every immigrant and cultural community across American history. And thus in that way, as in every other, this was by the time of the Spanish American and Philippine American wars an exemplary, longstanding, deeply rooted American culture.

The Filipino immigrants who arrived after those turn-of-the-twentieth-century conflicts certainly did so in greater numbers than any prior wave, and most came to distinct West Coast settings from those settled by the Louisiana Manila-men. But they also shared many impressive and inspiring experiences with those prior Filipino arrivals, exemplary, inclusive American stories that, like those of their Louisiana brethren, reflect just how fully the realities of this community counter and transcend the xenophobic, exclusionary fears to which they were too often subjected during these early-twentieth-century decades.

Many of those early Filipino American histories had involved military service, and within just the five-year period between 1910 and 1915, three twentieth-century Filipino Americans added their own achievements to that roster. In 1910, a twenty-two-year-old immigrant named Vicente Lim entered the U.S. Military Academy at West Point; although he faced significant prejudice, illustrated most succinctly by the nickname "Cannibal" bestowed upon him by his classmates, Lim would in 1914 become the first Filipino American West Point graduate. Upon graduation he was commissioned as the first Filipino officer for the Philippine Scouts, a U.S. military branch organized in the islands. Through the Scouts, Lim would be assigned to one of the three Filipino brigades mobilized during World War I, would pursue further military education over the next two decades, and during World War II would serve heroically as a brigadier general in the Philippine army during multiple conflicts with the Japanese. After the islands fell to the Japanese, Lim helped lead the Filipino resistance until his capture in 1944; he died while imprisoned by the Japanese. Lim was posthumously awarded both the Legion of Merit and a Purple Heart by the U.S. Army, in recognition of the crucial wartime contributions of this pioneering Filipino American officer.

During the same years that Lim was attending West Point, two other Philippine Scouts received their own groundbreaking, distinguished service medals from the U.S. Army. In February 1913, José Balitón Nísperos became the first Asian American to receive the Medal of Honor; the honor was awarded for his courageous service during the 1911 Moro Rebellion in the islands. And in April 1915, Telesforo de la Crux Trinidad became the first Asian American sailor to receive the Medal of Honor; his was awarded for heroic actions during a January 1915 boiler explosion and fire onboard the *U.S.S. San Diego* in Mexican waters. Nísperos received his medal in the Philippines and lived there for the remainder of his life; Trinidad received his in the United States, the nation for which he subsequently fought in both World War I and World War II. Those divergent stories, as well as the fact that Nísperos was fighting against fellow Filipinos, illustrate the different sides to Filipino and Filipino American communities in this complex early-twentieth-century period. But in truth, both men, like both settings and forms of Filipino community, were part of the United States, and both, like Vicente Lim, offered their heroic service to this nation despite the exclusionary fears and prejudice directed at them and their culture throughout this period.

Foundational community associations like La Sociedad de Beneficencia also had their echoes in this early-twentieth-century era. In 1912, Agripino M. Jaucian, a Filipino immigrant and former naval sailor living in Philadelphia, organized 200 fellow discharged U.S. Navy men into the Filipino American Association of Philadelphia, Inc. (FAAPI). Jaucian had experienced exclusionary racism and believed that such a communal association could both offer solidarity for members of the community and help them become a more thriving part of American society. After a few years of meeting informally in Jaucian's home, in 1917, FAAPI drafted a constitution and applied successfully for formal incorporation; the following year, it performed some of its most significant and heroic work, as Jaucian and his wife, Florence (a registered nurse), provided free medical supplies to Philadelphia residents fighting the devastating influenza epidemic of 1918. One hundred years after that moment, FAAPI remains in operation, the longest continually operating Filipino American organization; its work on the 2010 Smithsonian Exhibition *Singgalot, the Ties That Bind—Filipinos in America, From Colonial Subjects to Citizens* illustrates the group's commitment to preserving and strengthening collective memories of Filipino American history across the centuries.

The concentration of many of these early-twentieth-century Filipino arrivals in western U.S. communities of migrant labor led to new forms of inspiring communal organization and activism, ones that also produced corresponding new forms of exclusionary prejudice. The story of Pablo Manlapit and the first Filipino Labor Union (FLU) is particularly striking on both those levels. Manlapit was eighteen when he immigrated from the Philippines to Hawaii in 1909, one of the nearly 120,000 Filipinos to arrive in Hawaii between 1900 and 1931; he worked for a few years on the Hamakua Mill Company's sugarcane plantations, experiencing first hand some of the discriminations and brutalities of that labor world. In 1912, he married a

Hawaiian woman, Annie Kasby, and as they began a family he left the plantation world and began studying the law. By 1919, Manlapit had become a practicing labor lawyer, and he used his knowledge and connections to found the Filipino Labor Union on August 31, 1919; he was also elected the organization's first president. The FLU would organize major strikes on Hawaiian plantations in both 1920 and 1924, as well as complementary campaigns such as the 1922 Filipino Higher Wage Movement; these efforts did lead to wage increases and other positive effects, but the 1924 strike also culminated in the infamous September 9 Hanapepe Massacre, when police attacked strikers, killing nine and wounding many more.

Manlapit was one of sixty Filipino activists arrested after the massacre; as a condition of his parole he was deported to California in an effort to cripple Hawaiian labor organizing, but Manlapit continued his efforts in California, and in 1932 returned to Hawaii and renewed his activism there, hoping to involve Japanese, indigenous, and other local labor communities alongside Filipino laborers. In 1935, Manlapit was permanently deported from Hawaii to the Philippines, ending his labor movement career and tragically separating him from his family, but his influence and legacy lived on, both in Hawaii and in California. In Hawaii, the Filipino American activist Antonio Fagel organized a new, similarly cross-ethnic union, the Vibora Luviminda; the group struck successfully for higher wages in 1937, and would become the inspiration for an even more sizeable and enduring 1940s Hawaiian labor union begun by Chinese American longshoreman Harry Kamoku and others. In California, a group of Filipino American labor leaders would, in 1933 in the Salinas Valley, create a second Filipino Labor Union (also known as the FLU), immediately organizing a lettuce pickers' strike that received national media attention and significantly expanding the Depression-era conversation over Filipino and migrant laborers. In 1940, the American Federation of Labor chartered the Filipino-led Federal Agricultural Laborers Union, cementing these decades of activism into a formal and enduring labor organization.

The pensionados represented and helped create another new Filipino American community, one specific to this early-twentieth-century period. First envisioned by University of California professor Bernard Moses in 1900, created by the Philippine Commission (of which Moses was a founding member) in early 1903, and passed by Congress in August of that year, the Pensionado Act established an educational scholarship that would eventually allow nearly 14,000 Filipinos to travel to the United States and study at American colleges and universities (like the Chinese Educational Mission students, many of the pensionados also attended U.S. preparatory high schools). Both male and female students were included in the program, a significant element since otherwise the vast majority of Filipino immigrants to the United States during this era were male. While some pensionados remained in the United States after completing their schooling, most returned to the Philippines, becoming in the process some of their society's most influential educators and figures: national director of education Esteba Adaba (a University of Michigan alumnus); University of the Philippines president Jorge Bocobo (University of Indiana); Supreme Court chief justice and acting president during World War II José Abad Santos (an undergraduate degree from Northwestern and a masters in law from George Washington University); and many more. In 1919, less than a decade after his own graduation, Santos helped create the Philippines Women's University, Asia's first private nonsectarian women's college, reflecting just how broad and deep were the pensionados' educational and social legacies.

The Pensionado Act's successes also inspired many other Filipinos not affiliated with the program to pursue educational goals in the United States, and many of these did remain in the United States to further influence its society. By the 1920s, self-financed Filipino American students outnumbered pensionados; by 1930, Filipinos were the third largest community of students born outside the continental United States (after Chinese and Canadian students). These self-financed Filipino American students would become prominent in a number of social arenas during the era: labor leader Philip Vera Cruz, co-founder of the Agricultural Workers Organizing Committee that was a predecessor to the United Farm Workers, used his wages as a migrant laborer to attend Gonzaga University in the early 1930s; journalist Llamas Rosario received degrees from New York University and Columbia University, and in 1936, founded the Stockton (CA) *Filipino Pioneer*, the first Filipino American newspaper published in English and the self-described "national journal of Filipinos in America." From the military to the labor movement, education to the media, early-twentieth-century Filipino Americans extended and deepened the legacy and presence of this longstanding American community.

One of those hundreds of thousands of early-twentieth-century Filipino immigrants, an inconspicuous teenager who arrived in Seattle in 1930 and spent the next decade working among the Depression's burgeoning community of migrant laborers (Filipino American and beyond), would go on to write one of the most significant American literary works about these cultural and social communities, the Depression era, and inclusive definitions of America. Indeed, in both its title image and its culminating words this book captures that inclusive vision of American identity as clearly as any single text or document I've encountered.

Carlos Sampayan Bulosan was born into a farming family in Binalonan, in the Pangasinan province of the Philippines. As with many details of his early life there, his birthdate is uncertain, likely sometime between 1911 and 1913 (Bulosan frequently identifies 1911 in his writings, but his nephew and childhood friend Lorenzo Sampayan later set the date as November 2, 1913). In any case, after a childhood spent working alongside his family and experiencing significant poverty, he left for the United States as a young adult in July 1930, seeking new work opportunities and a different life. Like many Filipino immigrants, Bulosan arrived in Seattle, but over the next decade he would travel throughout the Pacific Northwest and California, finding consistent if precarious work as a migrant farm worker and laborer, for a time joining his brothers Aurelio and Lorenzo as dishwashers in San Luis Obispo, California, connecting to many other fellow Filipino American immigrants and communities, and experiencing a range of racist and exclusionary treatments from both public and official (such as police) and private and communal figures and voices.

Through both his own activist inclinations and the radicalization caused by experiencing those bigoted responses and abuses, Bulosan gradually became connected to the labor movement and other forms of political organizing and activism over these same years. His first piece of published writing likewise emerged out of those associations: in March 1943 he wrote an autobiographical and political essay inspired by the "Freedom from Want" section of President Franklin D. Roosevelt's 1941 "Four Freedoms" speech; and the *Saturday Evening Post* chose Bulosan's essay to accompany Norman Rockwell's famous painting *Freedom from Want*, the cover illustration for the March 6 issue of the magazine. The essay's first sentences establish its bold tone and public activist goals clearly: "If you want to know what we are, look upon the farms or upon the hard pavements of the city. You usually see us working or waiting for work, and you think you know us, but our outward guise is more deceptive than our history." Bulosan continues, "Our history has many strands of fear and hope that snarl and converge at several points in time and space," and the essay that follows moves between and across those more critical and more optimistic tones, ending on its most impassioned and inspiring note: "The America we hope to see is not merely a physical but also a spiritual and intellectual world. We are the mirror of what America is. If America wants us to be living and free, then we must be living and free. If we fail, then America fails."

Earlier in the essay Bulosan writes, "If you want to know what we are, look at the men reading books, searching in the dark pages of history for the lost word, the key to the mystery of the living peace." Three years later he would publish his own vital first book, an attempt to provide such key lost words, to offer stories and identities, communal narratives and individual perspectives, too often left out of history's dark pages. *America Is in the Heart* (1946) is at its core an autobiographical novel, a fictionalized retelling of Bulosan's own experiences from their starting points in the Philippines through his (at that point) fifteen years in the United States. But the book is much more than that, and in particular it combines critical and celebratory images of Filipino American experiences and community: like "Freedom from Want" it moves back and forth between the darkest and the most hopeful tones, and in so doing it offers some of our clearest literary depictions of both the exclusionary and the inclusive visions of American history and identity.

Even before he details his immigration to the United States, Bulosan foreshadows those exclusionary experiences, writing of Filipino beliefs in "false American ideals and modes of living." Just after he disembarks in Seattle, a young American girl says to her companion, "Look at those half-naked savages from the Philippines," and Bulosan calls the moment and other first experiences of xenophobic bigotry "the beginning of my life in America, the beginning of a long flight that carried me down the years, fighting desperately to find peace in some corner of life." Much of the book details those fights, conflicts that stem from many different sources—police brutality, mob violence, strike-breaking and other labor oppressions, and more—but that continually feature a core of what Bulosan calls "only violence and hate, living in a corrupt corner of America." And just as destructive as the exclusionary violence and hate are their effects on both Bulosan's own perspective and those of Filipino Americans more generally: of the first, he writes, "I had tried to keep my faith in America, but now I could no longer. It was broken, trampled upon, driving me out into dark nights with a gun in my hand"; and of the latter, he notes, "perhaps it was this narrowing of our life into an island, into a filthy segment of American society, that had driven Filipinos . . . inward, hating everyone and despising all positive urgencies toward freedom."

Yet those understandable low points are not the end, nor the heart, of Bulosan's American journey and vision. He had written of his first glimpse of Seattle that "it was like coming home after a long voyage, although as yet I had no home in this city. . . . With a sudden surge of joy, I knew that I must find a home in this new land." Although those hopes have been sorely tested by his experiences of a more exclusionary America, Bulosan finds a way to keep them alive, and comes in his book's concluding paragraph to its most optimistic and inclusive vision of his America:

> Then I heard bells ringing from the hills—like the bells that had tolled in the church tower when I had left Binalonan. I glanced out of the window again to look at the broad land I had dreamed so much about, only to discover with astonishment that the American earth was like a huge heart unfolding warmly to receive me. I felt it spreading through my being, warming me with its glowing reality. It came to me that no man—no one at all—could destroy my faith in America again. It was something that had grown out of my defeats and successes, something shaped by my struggles for a place in this vast land, digging my hands into the rich soil here and there, catching a freight to the north and to the south, seeking free meals in dingy gambling houses, reading a

book that opened up worlds of heroic thoughts. It was something that grew out of the sacrifices and loneliness of my friends, of my brothers in America and my family in the Philippines—something that grew out of our desire to know America, and to become a part of her great tradition, and to contribute something toward her final fulfillment. I knew that no man could destroy my faith in America that had sprung from all our hopes and aspirations, *ever*. (Bulosan's emphasis)

There are many inspiring moments and choices in that culminating paragraph, but I would end here by highlighting the linked pronouns in its final sentence: "my faith in America" and "our hopes and aspirations." What Bulosan's book illustrates most powerfully is a shared Filipino American experience and perspective, one too often circumscribed by exclusionary narratives but finding a way to return to an inclusive vision, building on the centuries of prior communities and histories and making clear that they, and their influence on America, will continue into the twenty-first century and beyond.

Chapter Seven

Everything Japanese Internment Got Wrong

No historical moment or national policy embodies the exclusionary definition of American identity and community more potently than does Japanese internment during World War II. The architects of this policy disregarded the gradual but noteworthy development of the Japanese American community over the prior half-century: there were about 2,300 Japanese Americans on the 1890 census; about 25,000 in 1900; and about 68,000 in 1910, with equivalent increases for the next few decades. None of those numbers reflected the even more significant and growing Japanese American population of Hawaii (which became a U.S. territory after its 1898 annexation but was not a state and so reported separately from those census reports): by 1920 the island's 110,000 Japanese Americans constituted 43 percent of Hawaii's total population; and as of 1930 there were more than 41,000 Japanese American schoolchildren in Hawaiian schools (out of 140,000 Japanese Hawaiians overall), to cite only two illustrations of this particularly sizeable Japanese American community.

If the internment policy failed to acknowledge that community's long-standing and evolving historical presence, it did build directly on exclusionary histories of bigotry and xenophobia directed at those Japanese Americans. The "Yellow Peril" fears and narrative that contributed so centrally to the 1882 Chinese Exclusion Act would soon be extended to the Japanese immigrants who (at least in part) took the place of those restricted Chinese arrivals in the nineteenth century's closing decades. In 1907, President Theodore Roosevelt negotiated a so-called gentlemen's agreement with the emperor of Japan, in which the United States promised not to legally restrict Japanese immigration if Japan pledged to stop issuing passports for immigration to the United States by single men (but continued to allow it for spouses and children of Japanese Americans). Although this agreement cut into Japanese immigration, it did not stop it entirely (particularly not for arrivals to Hawaii, for which Japan continued to issue passports), and so the United States did eventually include Japan in one of its most sweepingly exclusionary immigration laws: all Japanese arrivals were banned under the Asian Exclusion Act section of the Immigration Act of 1924 (also known as the Johnson-Reed Act and the Quota Act).

Just as the Chinese Exclusion Act and its follow-up laws did not destroy existing Chinese American communities (despite their overt goal of doing so), neither did these Japanese exclusions eliminate or even entirely restrict this evolving Japanese American community. The 1940 census reported just over 120,000 Japanese Americans living in the continental United States, with more than 25,000 of them foreign-born; the Japanese American population in Hawaii alone numbered another 158,000 in 1940. When Japanese forces bombed the U.S. naval base at Pearl Harbor on the morning of December 7, 1941, both the federal government specifically and American society more broadly were faced with a fundamental choice: whether to see this longstanding and growing Japanese American community as part of an inclusive national identity or to view them, through a xenophobic, exclusionary lens, as still owing allegiance to this foreign nation that was part of their collective heritage (in some cases many generations in the past, of course).

Unfortunately, and indeed very rapidly, the federal government adopted the exclusionary perspective. Executive Order 9066, issued by President Franklin D. Roosevelt on February 19, 1942 (less than seventy-five days after the Pearl Harbor attack), authorized the removal and indefinite internment of virtually all Japanese Americans living in the continental United States. Hawaii was initially exempt, due partly to the practical difficult of interning so many residents and partly to advocacy by local businessmen who recognized the vital contributions that tens of thousands of Japanese laborers made to their industries; besides eventually interning a couple thousand of its Japanese American residents, Hawaii did also implement a form of martial law, including a curfew and other restrictions for Japanese Americans, for much of the war.

The five-paragraph executive order mostly focuses on practicalities, but it features two especially telling choices: the concluding paragraph identifies the order as part of an ongoing series of presidential proclamations and actions (begun in the days immediately following Pearl Harbor) "prescribing regulations for the conduct and control of alien enemies"; and the long second paragraph, detailing the procedures by which the secretary of war and his military commanders will carry out the internment policy, discusses at particular length not the spaces to which Japanese Americans will be transported but instead those American places "from which any or all persons may be excluded." Even more clearly than the Chinese Exclusion Act or other exclusionary measures, this executive order defines an entire American community as an "alien" one in need of overt exclusion from many shared American spaces.

The executive order's effects were immediate, sweeping, and long-lasting. Well more than 110,000 Japanese Americans living in the continental United States (most on the West Coast) were, in the early months of 1942, removed to and imprisoned at more than sixty distinct facilities (of a number of different types and sizes) throughout the western and southwestern United States. More than 60 percent of those interned were American citizens, including such extreme situations as individuals with one-sixteenth Japanese ancestry; as Colonel Karl Bendetsen, the administrator of the wartime Civil Control Administration put it, "I am determined that if they have one drop of Japanese blood in them, they must go to camp." General John DeWitt, the commander of the Western Defense Command and an avowed white supremacist, put it more succinctly still: "A Jap's a Jap. It makes no difference whether the Jap is a citizen or not." In open testimony before Congress, DeWitt made plain the overtly and violently exclusionary purpose of the camps, as he saw them: "I don't want any of them here. . . . We must worry about the Japanese all the time until he is wiped off the map." And a *Los Angeles Times* editorial in support of internment linked the policy to a similarly exclusionary definition of American citizenship and identity: "So, a Japanese American born of Japanese parents, nurtured upon Japanese traditions, living in a transplanted Japanese atmosphere . . . notwithstanding his nominal brand of accidental citizenship almost inevitably and with the rarest exceptions grows up to be a Japanese, and not an American."

As a result of such sweepingly exclusionary attitudes and categorizations, nearly all Japanese Americans in the continental United States (and eventually about 2,000 in Hawaii), including the youngest of children, were removed and imprisoned as part of the internment process. Most of the camps and facilities remained in operation until 1945, meaning that the majority of detainees were interned for three years or more; a few camps, those which held so-called renunciants slated for deportation to Japan, remained open until early 1946. As the interned were generally allowed to bring only two suitcases of belongings each, most lost significant personal possessions; many also lost their jobs or livelihoods; and far too many even lost their homes or property, particularly the large number who had worked as tenant farmers prior to internment. At least seven detainees were killed in confrontations with camp guards, at least 1,800 died of diseases or other medical ailments while in the camps, and a vastly higher number (if not indeed all the interned) would suffer from psychological injuries and effects for the rest of their lives. Upon their return home many detainees were the victims of further exclusionary discrimination and violence; in one especially telling case, four white men brought to trial for attacking and setting fire to the Doi family farm in Placer County (California) in January 1945 were acquitted by a jury sympathetic to their claim that they were motivated by a desire to keep the United States "a white man's country."

In all these and many other ways, Japanese internment reflected both a coldly logical and a painfully destructive endpoint for exclusionary definitions of American identity. If members of a community were not truly Americans, it would stand to reason that their "alien" status could, under the wrong circumstances, render them not just outside of but distinctly hostile to the nation in which they lived. That logic had, after all, likewise motivated Revolutionary era fears of slave revolts, Jackson's Indian removal policy, restrictive and xenophobic immigration laws, legal support for Anglo squatters on Mexican American lands, and the many other historical exclusions I've traced in my prior chapters. But in no single moment had the exclusionary narrative operated with more clarity and force than when it produced, in the space of just a few short months and for a period of years thereafter, the removal and imprisonment of nearly 120,000 members of an American community.

Yet in the most exclusionary moments and histories, we find time and again examples of the most inclusive and inspiring visions of American identity. And indeed, just as I've highlighted for each of those other historical cases, Japanese internment produced a series of figures and stories that embody and exemplify an inclusive American community. From the man who worked tirelessly to challenge the internment policy, to the tens of thousands of men who demonstrated their patriotism and courage in the face of this xenophobic discrimination, to the future civil rights activists who turned their childhoods in internment camps into starting points for lives of communal service, these and other Japanese Americans modeled the best of American identity in the face of one of our darkest collective moments.

Fred Toyosaburo Korematsu (1919–2005) had just turned twenty-three years old when Executive Order 9066 was enacted. Korematsu had been born and raised in Oakland, to parents (Kakusaburo Korematsu and Kotsui Aoki) who had immigrated from Japan in 1905. Much of his early biography reads like that of any other American child and teenager: he attended Oakland public schools and was on the tennis and swim teams at Castlemont High School; he worked as a teenager at the family business, a flower nursey in San Leandro; he dated a classmate, Ida Boitano. But those same experiences were marred by anti-Japanese prejudice: Boitano's Italian American family disapproved of their relationship, believing the Japanese to be an inferior race; when military recruiters visited Castlemont High they told Korematsu "We have orders not to accept you" and refused to give him promotional materials; and he was summarily fired from his first two jobs after high school due to his Japanese heritage. As Korematsu later recounted these formative, exclusionary experiences, they helped prepare him both to expect and to resist discriminatory policies like Japanese internment.

On March 27, 1942, General DeWitt took the first step toward interning Japanese Americans in the Oakland area, restricting all Japanese Americans living in that region (known for internment purposes as Military Area No. 1) from leaving in anticipation of their removal. Just under six weeks later, on May 3, De Witt ordered all those Japanese American residents of the military area to report by May 9 to central gathering areas in order to be processed for internment. Korematsu was ready for these measures and took action to resist: going into hiding with Boitano; undergoing facial plastic surgery in order to repair an identifying broken nose and (as he later told investigators) more broadly to "change my appearance so that I would not be subject to ostracism when my girl and I went East"; and seeking to redefine his heritage as mixed Spanish and Hawaiian. But on May 30, police apprehended Korematsu on a street corner in San Leandro (he had been apparently trying to find work in the area in order to finance his and Boitano's escape east), and he was arrested and held in prison in San Francisco pending his transfer to an internment camp.

As those details about Korematsu and Boitano illustrate, Korematsu's initial resistance to internment was driven far more by his personal life and goals than by any broader civil rights agenda; there are of course few narratives more American than the desire to escape to new territory with a cross-cultural partner (a la Natty Bumppo and Chingachgook, Ishmael and Queequeg, Huckleberry Finn and Jim, etc.) of whom conservative traditions or older generations don't approve. But Korematsu did believe in a legal and philosophical principle underlying his resistance, the idea that "people should have a fair trial and a chance to defend their loyalty at court in a democratic way, because in this situation, people were placed in imprisonment without any fair trial." And when his case began to receive national media attention—as illustrated by a June 13, 1942, *New York Times* story headlined "3 JAPANESE DEFY CURBS; Army Says One Tried to Become 'Spaniard' by Plastic Surgery"—Korematsu would be given the chance to serve as a representative for such principles and for Japanese American resistance to the exclusionary policy and narratives of internment.

While he was in prison, Korematsu was contacted by Ernest Besig, founder and first director of the ACLU's northern California branch, about whether he would be willing to become a test case for legal resistance to internment. Besig was out on a limb in taking this position, as both a poll of northern California ACLU members and the organization's national office opposed these efforts to contest the constitutionality of Executive Order 9066. But Besig wrote to the ACLU executive director Roger Baldwin that "we feel compelled to proceed as before, because we cannot in good conscience withdraw from the case at this late date." Korematsu seems to have been aware of the stakes of Besig's support, later recalling that Besig "was sticking his neck out for me" because "at the time racial prejudice was pretty strong." Perhaps encouraged by this support, Korematsu agreed to serve as Besig's test case, and Besig (not himself a lawyer) recruited a friend, the fiery San Francisco attorney Wayne Collins, to represent Korematsu in his legal challenge.

Collins was perhaps more gifted as an orator and rhetorician than an attorney, and Korematsu lost his case at each judicial level. In September 1942, San Francisco federal judge Adolphus St. Sure found him guilty and sentenced him to five years' probation (although St. Sure seems to have done so reluctantly, as he initially refused to issue an order remanding Korematsu into military custody). After that initial guilty verdict, Korematsu was re-moved to the Central Utah War Relocation Center in Topaz, Utah, where he would remain for the duration of the war. A U.S. Court of Appeals agreed to hear his appeal in March 1943, but upheld the original verdict in a January 1944 decision. And the U.S. Supreme Court heard Collins's arguments in *Korematsu v. United States* in March 1944, but in December ruled 6–3 that compulsory exclusion was justified during circumstances of "emergency and peril." In his arguments before the Supreme Court, Collins demonstrated his rhetorical flair, arguing that "the only act resembling [internment] was com-mitted by Adolf Hitler, who penalized German citizens on the basis of their nationality." He convinced the three dissenters, as illustrated by Justice Owen Roberts's description of "the case [as] convicting a citizen as a punish-ment for not submitting to imprisonment in a concentration camp, based on his ancestry, and solely because of his ancestry," but the majority sided with the idea that such racial and national exclusions were temporarily necessary in wartime.

Yet while Korematsu did not win his legal battle nor escape from intern-ment, his resistance was an inspiring and influential one on multiple signifi-cant levels. Most immediately, it seems to have had a direct impact on another December 1944 Supreme Court decision that went the other way and helped limit and eventually end internment. Collins likewise represented that plaintiff, Mitsuye Endo, a twenty-two-year-old clerical worker who had filed a writ of habeas corpus to oppose her indefinite internment at the Tule Lake (California) camp. In Justice Hugo Black's majority opinion in *Korematsu* he overtly cites *Ex parte Mitsuye Endo*, arguing that "the *Endo* case graphically illustrates the difference between the validity of an order to exclude and the validity of a detention order after exclusion has been effected." Not at all coincidentally, the Court released its unanimous decision in support of Endo's writ on the same day (December 18, 1944) it did *Korematsu*. Writing for the Court in *Endo*, Justice William Douglas notes that "We are of the view that Mitsuye Endo should be given her liberty," adding, "whatever power the War Relocation Authority may have to detail other classes of citizens, it has no authority to subject citizens who are concededly loyal to its leave procedure." The Court's duality in response to Korematsu and Endo is frustrating, but nonetheless the Endo decision represented a significant step in opposing internment, and Korematsu's case clearly factored into it.

For a few decades after his release from the Topaz camp, Korematsu disappeared into the private life he had long desired; he continued to face anti-Japanese prejudice, but also moved to Detroit, married Kathryn Pearson in October 1946, moved back to Oakland with her when his mother became ill in 1949, and had two children over the next few years. But when he reentered public and legal conversations in the early 1980s, it comprised another layer to his case's influential legacy and effects. Peter Irons, a lawyer and professor at the University of California, San Diego, was researching a book on internment and discovered evidence that the U.S. solicitor general who argued *Korematsu* before the Supreme Court had withheld FBI and military reports, which concluded that Japanese Americans posed no security risk. Irons brought a writ of error before San Francisco federal court judge Marilyn Hall Patel, and persuaded Korematsu to testify in the proceeding that he could vacate his original conviction. Korematsu did so eloquently, arguing that "I would like to see the government admit that they were wrong and do something about it so this will never happen again to any American citizen of any race, creed, or color," and adding, "If anyone should do any pardoning, I should be the one pardoning the government for what they did to the Japanese-American people." On April 19, 1984, Patel formally vacated Korematsu's conviction, an important legal step that helped pave the way for future victories including (especially) the Civil Liberties Act of 1988, which provided financial reparations for each surviving detainee.

Those individual and collective results would have been more than enough to cement Korematsu's legacy and impact, but in the last years of his life he took his public activism one significant step further still. After the September 11, 2001, terrorist attacks, Korematsu became an outspoken advocate for civil liberties and critic of many of the War on Terror's infringements of such rights. In particular, he filed two amicus curiae briefs to accompany Supreme Court cases involving detainees at the Guantanamo Bay prison: an October 2003 brief for the cases of Shafiq Rasul and Khaled Al Odah, in which Korematsu cites numerous historical examples (including but not limited to Japanese internment) to argue that the restriction of civil liberties is never justified; and an April 2004 brief for Jose Padilla's case, in which Korematsu parallels his own internment situation to that of Padilla and argues, "full vindication for the Japanese-Americans will arrive only when we learn that, even in times of crisis, we must guard against prejudice and keep uppermost our commitment to law and justice." Through these impressive twenty-first-century briefs and activist efforts, the second drafted less than a year before his March 2005 death, Korematsu ensured that his own history, story, and legal battle would continue to echo into a new era of exclusionary restrictions and inclusive alternatives.

Korematsu and his fellow plaintiff, Mitsuye Endo, were far from the only Japanese Americans who offered such inclusive alternatives during the internment era. Complementing those individual acts of legal resistance was the collective patriotism, bravery, and service of the more than 33,000 Japanese Americans who comprised a trio of all-Japanese U.S. Army units in the course of World War II (among many other avenues through which Japanese Americans contributed to the armed forces and war effort). These soldiers, many of whom volunteered out of the internment camps themselves and all of whom represented a potent challenge to the narratives and logic behind the camps, became some of the war's most praised and decorated forces and exemplify the best of what an inclusive America can be.

Just a month after Pearl Harbor, and long before the formation of any of those three Japanese American units, there was the Varsity Victory Volunteers. Immediately following the attack, ROTC students throughout Hawaii reported for duty as the newly formed Hawaii Territorial Guard (HTG), but when the authorities in Washington learned of Japanese Americans within the HTG, they dismissed those students as "enemy aliens" (military category 4C). The frustrated students consulted with Hung Wai Ching, a Chinese American minister and community leader who had become an ally to the local Japanese American community, and he encouraged them to offer their services as a labor battalion. The students wrote a letter to the territory's military governor, Delos Emmons, which read,

> We, the undersigned, were members of the Hawaii Territorial Guard until its recent inactivation. We joined the Guard voluntarily with the hope that this was one way to serve our country in her time of need. Needless to say, we were deeply disappointed when we were told that our services in the Guard were no longer needed. Hawaii is our home; the United States, our country. We know but one loyalty and that is to the Stars and Stripes. We wish to do our part as loyal Americans in every way possible and we hereby offer ourselves for whatever service you may see fit to use us.

Their inclusive vision convinced Emmons, and in February 1942 the Varsity Victory Volunteers (VVV) was formed.

For the next year, the VVV was assigned to Honolulu's Schofield Barracks, serving under the 34th Combat Engineers Regiment in the U.S. Army Corps of Engineers. Working for shelter and food and virtually no pay, the VVV performed a number of important duties at the barracks, from building roads to stringing barbed wire fences, working the nearby quarry to constructing military installations. They also became close to the other soldiers stationed at Schofield, even forming football, basketball, boxing, and golf teams that competed against their fellow soldiers. This year of shared service was vital to the rest of the Japanese American war effort: as Hawaiian historian Gwenfread Allen writes,

> It was the VVV which marked the turning point in the treatment of the people of Japanese ancestry in this Territory and their acceptance by the rest of the community. What followed afterward . . . was the natural result of the trend which was started in the early months of the war when a group of young men, who numbered at no time more than 170, demonstrated to a suspicious and skeptical community that the Americans of Japanese ancestry were every bit as American and every bit as loyal to this country and to her ideals as any other group of Americans, whether they were white, yellow, black, or brown.

The VVV also contributed directly to the policy shift that produced the all-Japanese American military units. Throughout 1942, the federal government and military commanders continued to categorize all Japanese American soldiers and volunteers as 4C (enemy aliens), extending the exclusionary narrative of the internment camps to these members of the armed forces as well. In December 1942, assistant secretary of war John McCloy visited the island of Oahu to tour its military facilities; when he reached Schofield, Hung Wai Ching, his local escort, made sure to point out VVV members at work, living among their comrades in the barracks, serving as part of every aspect of this successfully inclusive, multicultural facility. Just a few weeks later, in early January 1943, the War Department reversed its exclusionary policy and announced plans to create two all Japanese American combat units, the 100th Infantry Battalion and the 442nd Regimental Combat Team. The members of the VVV requested official permission to disband so they could join the new units; on January 31 the VVV was disbanded, and its soldiers were among the 10,000 Hawaiian Japanese Americans to volunteer for the 100th and 442nd in their first months of existence.

The 100th was the first unit to assemble, initially at Wisconsin's Fort McCoy and then for full combat training at Mississippi's Fort Shelby. While the majority of its initial group of roughly 5,000 soldiers came from among those 10,000 Hawaiian volunteers, more than 1,000 members volunteered from the mainland's internment camps, in one of American history's most overt and stunning examples of an inclusive vision of America countering and transcending exclusionary narratives and policies. When the battalion received its colors in late July 1943, they came with the motto "Remember Pearl Harbor," at the unit's request. After a few months of training the 100th shipped out in August 1943 to North Africa, landing there and then crossing the Mediterranean to take part in the September 1943 through June 1944 Allied invasion of Italy and liberation of Rome. The battalion fought with particular distinction, taking casualties at a high rate, gaining the informal nickname "The Purple Heart Battalion," and garnering consistent recognition and acclaim from their commanders and the military authorities (including 21 Medals of Honor, the highest award for combat valor, awarded to members of the 100th).

If the 100th made clear all that Japanese American soldiers could bring to the Allied forces and war effort, the experiences of the 442nd (into which the 100th was folded once the full regiment was assembled) amplified those histories significantly. That included exclusionary bigotry, as the regiment was initially met in Hattiesburg, Mississippi (home to Fort Shelby), by signs and editorials that read "Japs not wanted" and "Go home Japs." But Hung Wai Ching, who after his work with the VV had adopted the 442nd as a new cause, spoke to the town's chief of police and newspaper editor, explaining that "these boys were all Americans and that they had all volunteered to serve their country," and the overt exclusionary propaganda mostly disappeared. And after completing training at Shelby and shipping to Italy on May 1, 1944, to join the 100th Battalion, the 442nd would spend the next year fighting as courageously and impressively as any U.S. military unit ever had. It was the 442nd that in the winter of 1944 was sent in to successfully rescue the so-called Lost Battalion of Texans who had been surrounded by German forces in the Vosges Mountains; the 442nd that in April 1945 (by special request of General Mark Clark) broke through the Gothic Line in northern Italy that had resisted Allied advances for six months; and the 442nd that sent the soldiers in its 522nd Field Artillery Battalion to support the May 1945 final invasion of Germany, with men of the 522nd liberating the concentration camp at Dachau in the process.

For those and many other heroic efforts, the 442nd—which suffered an extremely high rate of casualties, with more than 800 soldiers killed or missing in action—would become the most decorated U.S. army unit in American history. Its soldiers received over 4,000 Purple Hearts, 29 Distinguished Service Crosses, 588 Silver Stars, and more than 4,000 Bronze Stars in just a single year of combat. The 442nd also received seven Distinguished Unit Citations, with the last awarded personally by President Truman in July 1946. "You fought the enemy abroad and prejudice at home and you won," Truman remarked as he awarded this final citation to this most decorated military unit. And indeed, while those battles were of course distinct in many ways, they were both fought against by exclusionary forces, those who would define certain cultures and communities as alien to a society and seek to remove and imprison them as a result. The men of the 100th and 442nd refused to accept such xenophobic bigotry, defining themselves instead as central parts of their nation through their service and sacrifice.

By the war's end, approximately 30,000 Japanese Americans had served in the U.S. military, including 18,000 in the 442nd and 6,000 in the military intelligence service (another arena in which Japanese American volunteers proved invaluable). The service of these men and women was impressive and heroic on its own terms, and needs no further context to be commemorated and celebrated than that. Yet at the same time, the juxtaposition of this exemplification of an inclusive American community, one in which every ethnic and cultural group forms a vital part without which the nation might not endure and certainly would not prosper, with one of the most overtly exclusionary periods in American history is both ironic and deeply telling. If the internment policy and camps represented one of the most blatant expressions of the exclusionary vision America had ever enacted, then out of the same moment—and even at times the same camps—came one of the most inspiring models for an alternative, inclusive vision of the nation.

Out of the internment camps came as well many young Americans, children who had spent formative years in this exclusionary prison and who, as I noted above, would inevitably bear the effects of those experiences for the rest of their lives. Yet without minimizing in any way those difficult and traumatic realities, it's important to note that some of the most impressive and inspiring late-twentieth- and twenty-first-century Americans were children in the internment camps. Here I'll highlight two, one who contributed greatly to the civil rights struggles of the 1960s and beyond, and one who has contributed significantly to those unfolding in our own twenty-first-century moment.

Yuri Kochiyama (1921–2014) was born Mary Yuriko Nakahara to two Japanese immigrants, Seeichi and Tsuyako Nakahara, in San Pedro, California. As with Fred Korematsu, Mary's first couple of decades of life were very typical: as a teenager she taught Sunday school at her family's Presbyterian Church; she was the first female student body officer (class vice president) and a journalist and tennis player at San Pedro High School, graduating in 1939; and she received a degree in English from Compton Junior College in 1941. But her and her family's lives changed drastically after Pearl Harbor, and indeed long before internment. Her father, who had just returned from a hospital stay for ulcer surgery, was arrested by the FBI on the same day as the Pearl Harbor attack for suspicious ties to Japanese officials (such as the ambassador to the U.S., Kichisaburō Nomura); he was detained for six weeks before being cleared, his medical issues worsening all the while, and on January 21, 1942, the day after his release, he passed away.

That family tragedy would be extended after Executive Order 9066. Yuri and her family were removed not long after the order, first spending a few months at the Santa Anita Assembly Center (sleeping in a converted horse stable) and then being interned for three years at a camp in Jerome, Arkansas. Yet Yuri turned that internment experience from exclusionary and isolating to inclusive and connecting, building on her prior experiences to help create a multilayered Japanese American community. She organized her young Japanese American Sunday school students, known as the Crusaders, which spread across a number of internment camps, to send letters and care packages to Japanese American soldiers, including Yuri's twin brother Peter. The conversations enhanced the feeling of community for those at the camps as well as soldiers, an effect amplified when Yuri printed some of the soldiers' replies in her Jerome camp newspaper column, "Nisei in Khaki." And they also led to a turning point in Yuri's own life, as she met and married one such soldier, Bill Kochiyama.

Over the remainder of the twentieth and into the twenty-first century, Yuri and Bill would pursue civil rights and political activism on behalf of both their own and many other communities. During the Civil Rights era they joined Asian Americans for Action, a pioneering group founded in 1969 in New York City (where the couple had moved after the war) and modeled on the Black Panthers, and helped spearhead the group's antiwar and anti-imperialist efforts. And Yuri and Bill's subsequent work on behalf of American collective memories of and engagement with internment was critical to the move toward the 1988 Civil Liberties Act. In the early 1980s, the couple helped organize Concerned Japanese Americans and East Coast Japanese Americans for Redress, through both groups advocating for making New York a site for one of the Commission on Wartime Relocation and Internment of Civilians (CWRIC) hearings. They succeeded, and at the hearings the combination of Bill's official testimony and Yuri's display of political art helped raise awareness for the commission's efforts and move the national conversation toward legal and financial reparations for internment.

Yuri in particular was also extremely active in other civil rights and activist movements during and after the 1960s. After the couple and their six children moved to Harlem, Yuri became active in the African American community and civil rights activism, and in October 1963, after she had been arrested as part of a protest, met and befriended Malcolm X. She introduced Malcolm to visiting Japanese Hibakusha (atomic bomb survivors), became active in his Organization of Afro-American Unity, and was present at his February 1965 assassination in Harlem's Audobon Ballroom; a famous *Life* magazine photograph of the tragedy shows Yuri cradling Malcolm's body in her arms after the shooting. She would remain active in the civil rights and African American rights movements long after this tragedy and would expand her efforts to other communities as well, most famously in her participation in a 1977 takeover of the Statue of Liberty by Puerto Rican protesters advocating for Puerto Rican independence and the release of political prisoners.

That latter action, as well as Yuri's vocal support for such controversial figures as Fidel Castro and Ho Chi Minh (among other controversies in her long activist life), might seem to locate her in opposition to the United States. Yet while she certainly and consistently criticized, and at times overtly opposed, the U.S. government and its policies, such dissent is both (to quote Howard Zinn) the highest form of patriotism and a natural legacy of her World War II experiences with official, anti-Japanese xenophobia and internment. Indeed, I would argue that Yuri's political and social protests exist on a spectrum with Bill's military service and Fred Korematsu's legal resistance, all representing forms of Japanese American challenge to both the policies and the narratives of internment. If Yuri's inclusive vision took the form of solidarity with other American (and global) communities in their shared struggle for freedom and rights, that's just as valuable a contribution to civic life as those other forms.

George Hosato Takei (1937–) experienced internment at a much younger age than Yuri but has built a similar multifaceted, inclusive life of communal activism and artistic achievement upon that exclusionary foundation. Born in Los Angeles to an American-born mother (Fumiko Nakamura) and Japanese immigrant father (Takekuma Takei), George was removed with his family before his fifth birthday. After spending months at the same Santa Anita horse-park-turned-assembly-center as Yuri's family, the Takeis were interned, first in Rohwer, Arkansas, and then at the infamous Tule Lake center in California. As Takei documented the family's move to Tule Lake in a 2017 *New York Times* op ed, "My mother and father's only crime was refusing, out of principle, to sign a loyalty pledge promulgated by the government. The authorities had already taken my parents' home on Garnet Street in Los Angeles, their once thriving dry cleaning business, and finally their liberty. Now they wanted them to grovel; this was an indignity too far." And so they were removed yet again to Tule Lake, "the harshest camp, with more than 18,500 inmates behind three layers of barbed-wire fence and with tanks patrolling the perimeter."

After surviving Tule Lake and internment, Takei returned to resume a normal childhood and young adult life: attending junior high and then high school in Los Angeles; joining the pioneering Boy Scout Troop 379 at the city's Koyasan Buddhist Temple; graduating from UCLA with a bachelor of arts degree (1960) and then a master's degree (1964) in theater. By that time he had been working in Hollywood for nearly a decade, and in 1964 had a starring role in "The Encounter," a *Twilight Zone* episode in which he played the tortured son of a Japanese American man who collaborated with Japanese pilots during the Pearl Harbor attack. The following year he was cast in a truly groundbreaking role, not only in his own career but also for Asian Americans in Hollywood: Lt. Hikaru Sulu, a Japanese American officer on the original *Star Trek*'s *USS Enterprise*. While of course *Star Trek* is set in a distant future and far from Earth, it famously depicts, in its core cast as well as its plotlines and worldview, an inclusive, peaceful vision of community. And as Takei recounts his conversations with creator Gene Roddenberry, Sulu specifically reflected those inclusive visions, most clearly in that surname: Roddenberry wanted the character to represent Asia as a whole, and so named him after the Sulu Sea, since "the waters of that sea touch all shores."

Takei played the character of Sulu in the original TV series, an early 1970s animated series, the first six *Star Trek* feature films, and many other projects. He will forever be associated with the role, and seems more than fine with that. But in the last two decades he has also turned his attention and efforts to civil rights and political activism, on a couple of distinct fronts. In 2005, Takei publicly came out as gay, the culminating moment in a process he described as "more like a long, long walk through what began as a narrow corridor that starts to widen." That public declaration was prompted directly by a civil rights challenge: California governor Arnold Schwarzenegger's veto of a same-sex marriage law. And in the years since Takei has consistently used his platform and celebrity to advocate for gay rights, from his 2006 "Equality Trek" tour to his recording of public service announcements (PSAs) opposing antigay voices and policies to his current role as a principal spokesperson for the Human Rights Campaign's "Coming Out Project." In one of those PSAs, recorded in 2011 to oppose a Tennessee law forbidding public school teachers and students from referring to homosexuality in any way, Takei even offered his name as a substitute for "gay," as in "Takei marriage" or "Takei Pride parades." That gesture alone reflects an inclusive perspective, one which puts his personal identity in direct relationship to this communal battle for recognition and rights and in so doing thoroughly and significantly links Takei to all his fellow gay Americans.

One year later, Takei likewise lent both his personal identity and his artistic clout to the groundbreaking musical *Allegiance*. The show's creators, Jay Kuo and Lorenzo Thione, were inspired directly by meeting Takei and hearing his stories of internment, and they built upon those personal and communal histories to create their story of the fictional Kimura family's experiences at Wyoming's Heart Mountain internment camp (this version of which features many elements of the Tule Lake camp). The show's plot features elements of each of the histories I've highlighted in this chapter, from a main character who serves in the 442nd Regimental Combat Team to acts of legal and social resistance and communal activism, both outside and inside the internment camps. Takei took part in every stage of the show's development, from its July 2009 first reading at the Japanese American National Museum in Los Angeles to a crowd-sourced funding campaign on his Facebook page to performing in two central roles in both the September 2012 San Diego debut and the October 2015 Broadway premiere. Takei has called the show, one of the first works of mainstream popular culture to focus on the histories of internment, his legacy project.

While *Allegiance* certainly does represent an important cultural representation of the internment policy and era, it is Takei himself who, like Yuri and Bill Kochiyama, like Fred Korematsu and Matsuye Endo, and like the soldiers of the 442nd, best embodies the legacies of that period. Perhaps the single most exclusionary moment in American history, and yet a moment out of which so many inclusive stories, figures, and activisms emerged. A moment in which the allegiance and American identity of a community were questioned and attacked, and yet American ideals were reaffirmed and exemplified by that same Japanese American community.

Chapter Eight

There's Nothing New about Muslim Americans

In the first two decades of the twenty-first century, the most consistent and blatant exclusionary narratives have been those directed at Muslim Americans. Such Islamophobic exclusions certainly existed prior to the turn of the new century as well, as illustrated with particular clarity by the caricatured stereotypical Muslim terrorist villains of popular American action films like Arnold Schwarzenegger's *True Lies* (1994) or Kurt Russell and Halle Berry's *Executive Decision* (1996). But it was after the September 11, 2001, terrorist attacks that these fearful, violent, and exclusionary attitudes and responses to Muslim Americans truly became a dominant presence in American society. To cite one particularly alarming trend, according to FBI data, the number of reported anti-Muslim hate crimes jumped from 28 in 2000 to 481 in 2001 (with most of them likely occurring in the few months after September 11); while the number "fell" to 155 in 2002, it remained above 100 for every year between 2002 and 2014 (and has surged once more in recent years, with 257 in 2015 and 307 in 2016). These troubling contemporary numbers echo but also extend and amplify the kinds of collective, exclusionary violence directed at Chinese Americans in the late nineteenth century and Filipino Americans in the early twentieth century, to cite two of my prior chapters' focal exclusionary histories.

Accompanying, directly contributing to, and in some key ways extending beyond these violent responses has been an emerging narrative that defines Muslim Americans—not just Muslims in other nations like the Al Qaeda terrorists, but Muslim Americans here in the United States—as distinctly foreign and even hostile to the United States. This narrative took a variety of forms throughout the early 2000s, but was particularly apparent in the dual and interconnected conspiracy theories directed at Barack Obama when he first ran for president in 2008. The so-called Birther movement that sought to define Obama as secretly foreign-born drew the most attention, but just as influential was the narrative that Obama was also secretly Muslim. As late as 2015, an astoundingly high percentage of registered GOP voters believed then-President Obama to be a Muslim: 43 percent in a September 2015 CNN poll and 54 percent in a Public Policy Polling poll from that same month. The coexistence of these two outrageously inaccurate conspiracy theories about Obama reveals also their overlap, the way in which "foreign" and "Muslim" could become, if not synonymous, at least closely tied to one another in such exclusionary narratives. When, in response to vice presidential nominee Sarah Palin's repeated query, "Who is the real Barack Obama?" during 2008 campaign rallies, audience members responded with "terrorist" and "traitor," they were offering one more illustration of the link between stereotypical Muslim terrorists, foreigners, and enemies of the United States.

These Islamophobic exclusionary narratives were further amplified during the 2016 presidential campaign. Presidential candidate Ben Carson remarked in September 2015 that before a Muslim American would be able to become president, he or she would have to "renounce Islam," and the long-standing and popular syndicated newspaper columnist Cal Thomas seconded that notion in a follow-up piece, arguing that "avoiding a Muslim in the White House is caution, not bigotry." In that same month, Irving, Texas, mayor Beth Van Duyne defended that city's arrest of a fourteen-year-old Muslim American student, Ahmed Muhammed (for assembling a homemade clock for science class that was mistaken for a terrorist bomb), linking it to her conspiratorial opposition to a fictional "Sharia law court" in the state and wondering, "Why am I not one of many who when I see something, I say something? Why are we not all holding all of our elected officials accountable for saying the things that we're all thinking?" And also in that same month, the *New York Times* profiled South Carolina residents opposed to accepting Syrian refugees into their communities and state, quoting a local businessman, Jim McMillan, as arguing, "The U.N. calls it 'refugee resettlement'—the Muslims call it hijra [usually spelled "hegira"], migration. They don't plan to assimilate, they don't plan to take on our culture. They plan to change the way of American life."

The November 2016 election of Donald Trump to the presidency has brought those anti-Muslim exclusionary narratives even more to the fore of both national policies and communal conversations. As early as November 16 of that year, Trump surrogate and advisor Carl Higbie argued on Fox News that a proposed registry of Muslim Americans would be legally upheld, noting, "To be perfectly honest, it is legal. They say it will hold constitutional muster. I know the ACLU is going to challenge it, but I think it'll pass. . . . We did it during World War II with the Japanese. . . . I'm just saying there is precedent for it." While President Trump has not yet followed through on that idea, one of his most consistent policy proposals and objectives has been to institute a Muslim Exclusion Act by another name, the "Muslim ban" immigration proposal that has gone through numerous iterations, court challenges and limits, and renewed efforts. As of June 2018, the most recent version of this "travel ban" (as the administration has attempted to categorize it, although both Trump and legal advisors like Rudy Giuliani have overtly referred to it as a Muslim ban on multiple occasions) was upheld by the Supreme Court in a 5–4 decision; while this iteration extended the banned arrivals to North Koreans and specific Venezuelan government officials, those were miniscule changes to a proposal that continues to focus on excluding immigration and travel to the United States from five predominantly Muslim countries (Iran, Libya, Somalia, Syria, and Yemen).

These exclusionary proposals and policies have once again been complemented by broader Islamophobic narratives and hate crimes. In March 2018, the think tank New America produced a data visualization project that traced anti-Muslim laws, rhetoric, and violence in a handful of distinct categories since 2012, including "anti-Sharia legislation," community rejections of planned mosques and other Muslim American construction projects, and anti-Muslim hate crimes, among other types. They found a significant spike in all categories since 2015, with, for example, 87 percent of the documented hate crimes taking place since mid-2015. In July 2018, the Council on American-Islamic Relations (CAIR) produced a report about the year's second quarter (April through June), during which CAIR had received 1,006 reports of potential anti-Muslim "bias incidents" and had determined through investigation that 431 of them contained "an identifiable element of anti-Muslim bias." One consistent thread across such incidents (and those directed at other Americans possibly mistaken for Muslim, such as Sikh Americans) has been rhetoric that identifies these individuals as foreign, as illustrated by the August 2018 beating of a Sacramento Sikh American man by a mob shouting "You're not welcome here" and "Go back to your country."

That narrative is a key thread across all of these early twenty-first century anti-Muslim exclusions. Time and again, Muslim Americans have been defined as a new, threatening, foreign community and culture, as fundamentally different from and outside of the "America" being envisioned in these definitions. That's become a dominant narrative not only for new immigrants and arrivals, but also and perhaps especially for Muslims already in the United States, as exemplified by the constant fears of existing Muslim American communities instituting and practicing "Sharia law." Seen through this exclusionary Islamophobic lens, Muslims can never become part of a nation that is not Muslim-majority or overtly Islamic in its government, and thus, in this increasingly prominent early twenty-first-century definition, Muslim

Americans will always remain foreign and threatening to American identity and community.

One particularly clear and crucial way to challenge that twenty-first-century exclusionary narrative, then, is to highlight the presence and contribution of Muslim American individuals and communities across American history. Muslim Americans have been part of each stage of the American story, sometimes as striking individual figures, sometimes as part of larger communities, but in each and every case constituting elements of a longstanding, foundational American culture. An inclusive vision of American identity wouldn't be complete without these originating and consistent Muslim American presences.

To start with the community's (and in many ways, the nation's) origin point: historians estimate that between 15 percent and 30 percent of the African slaves transported to North America over the two centuries of the transatlantic slave trade were Muslim. Even at the low end of that estimated number, that would mean something like 2 million Muslims came to the continent in this way, a religious and cultural community comparable to most of the significant European immigrant communities over these same centuries. These Muslim African arrivals constituted a sizeable enough contingent that a 1682 Virginia law delineating those cultural communities who could legally be held as slaves in the colony listed "Moors" (Muslim North Africans) second after "Negroes." Certainly many of these millions of Muslim slaves subsequently converted (or, more exactly, were forced to convert) to Christianity, and in any case, tracing any factors in the heritages and identities of African American slaves across the centuries of the slave system is a fraught and fragile historical process at best. Yet just as African American slaves overall contributed immeasurably to the culture and identity of America throughout these formative centuries, so too did these Muslim American slaves specifically influence the community's development in countless ways.

Included among these millions of early Muslim African slaves was one of the first individually known, and even famous, arrivals to the Americas. One of the three companions who traveled with Álvar Nuñez Cabeza de Vaca in his eight-year journey across the continent (about which I wrote in chapter 1) was Estevanico (c. 1500–1539), a Moorish Muslim slave also known as Esteban the Moor and Mustafa Azemmouri. Estevanico had been sold into slavery in 1522 in the Portuguese-controlled Moroccan coastal town of Azemmour, and ended up enslaved to a Spanish nobleman, Andrés Dorantes de Carranza. Carranza brought Estevanico on the 1527 Narváez expedition as a slave, but once that expedition collapsed and Estevanico found himself part of de Vaca's small cohort of survivors (de Vaca writes in his narrative that "the fourth [survivor] is Estevanico, an Arab Negro from Azamor"), the four men became very much peers for the remainder of their time on the continent. When that eight-year trek was over, Estevanico remained in the Americas, serving as a guide for first the viceroy of New Spain (Antonio de Mendoza) and then for the explorer Friar Marcos de Niza. Estevanico disappeared while leading de Niza's 1539 expedition among the Zuni tribe in present-day New Mexico—possibly killed by the Zuni, possibly gaining his freedom, and in any case, adding one more layer to the legend of this pioneering early Muslim American life.

Estevanico's striking individual life and contributions to the contact and exploration era foreshadowed the stories and influences of other prominent Muslim American individuals across significant stages in early American history. At least a handful of Muslim American colonists are known to have fought for the Continental Army during the Revolutionary War, including Bampett Muhamed (a freedman who served as a corporal with the Virginian forces), Yusuf ben Ali (a slave also known as Joseph Benhaley, who fought with General Thomas Sumter in South Carolina), Salem Poor and Peter Salem (two former slaves who fought at the June 1775 Battle of Charleston/ Bunker Hill in Massachusetts) and Joseph Saba (a fifer with George Washington's Continental troops). Of Salem Poor in particular, a group of his fellow Minutemen would draft a December 1775 petition to the General Court of the Massachusetts Bay Colony testifying to his exemplary service in that crucial early Revolutionary battle, writing, "We declare that a Negro man called Salem Poor of Col. Frye's Regiment, Capt. Ames Company in the late Battle of Charleston, behaved like an experienced officer, as well as an excellent officer, to set forth particulars of his conduct would be tedious. We would only beg leave to say in the person of this Negro centers a brave & gallant Soldier."

As the new nation moved into the Early Republic stage after the Revolution, Muslim Americans continued to occupy prominent individual and communal roles. Yarrow Mamout (Muhammad Yaro) was sold into slavery from the West African nation of Guinea in 1752 (when he was sixteen years old) and brought to Annapolis, Maryland. He was enslaved on the Beall plantation in nearby Takoma Park, Maryland, and became well known as a handyman and brick maker; eventually he established a sufficient reputation and savings that the Beall family entered into a financial agreement with him and he was able to purchase his freedom in April 1807. He would go on to become a homeowner, investor, and community leader in the Georgetown area of Washington, DC, and a famous enough figure that the prominent Early Republic artist Charles Willson Peale painted a portrait of Mamout in 1819. As Peale wrote, "Yarrow owns a House & lotts and is known by most of the Inhabitants of Georgetown. . . . He professes to be a mahometan [Muslim], and is often seen & heard in the Streets singing Praises to God."

During the same Early Republic period, another Muslim slave from Guinea, Bilali Muhammad, contributed significantly to both the new nation and the emerging Muslim American community. Muhammad was likewise sold into slavery as a teenager (in the 1780s) and brought to the Caribbean, where he was sold to the Middle Caicos plantation of an English loyalist emigrant from America named Dr. Bell. Around 1802, Bell sold him to a Georgia planter named Thomas Spalding, who due to Muhammad's literacy and fluency in Arabic (apparently a common language among Spalding's slaves), as well as his overall leadership qualities, made him head driver on his Sapelo Island plantation. During the War of 1812, Sapelo Island came under attack, and Muhammad and the 500 or so slaves he oversaw played a crucial role in successfully defending the island for the United States. Sometime before his 1857 death, Muhammad would also write an important early Muslim American and American text: this thirteen-page treatise, known alternately as the *Bilali Muhammad Document* and the *Ben Ali Diary* (although it has no autobiographical elements), details Islamic beliefs and practices, presumably as a guide for Muhammad's fellow Muslim Americans.

Another early Muslim American text, the 1831 autobiography of Umar (or Omar) ibn Sayyid, was even more overtly shared in an effort to create a burgeoning Muslim American community. Sayyid was from the Fulani people in the West African nation of Futa Toro (modern Senegal), and was captured into slavery sometime around 1807 (when he was in his thirties). He was brought to Charleston, enslaved to a brutal master there from whom he escaped to Fayetteville, North Carolina, in August 1810, and recaptured, imprisoned, and eventually sold to a kinder master, James Owen of Bladen County. Owen, a devout Presbyterian, purchased Sayyid both a Qur'an in English and a Bible in Arabic, in order to help Sayyid learn English but also to discuss religion with him in an effort to convert him to Christianity. It's unclear whether Owen succeeded, but in any case, Sayyid remained committed to expressing his Muslim American identity and through it building a Muslim American community: in 1831 he wrote a fifteen-page autobiography in Arabic, and in 1836 he sent a copy of it to Lamine Kebe, a freed Muslim American slave living in New York City. Kebe, known in the city as "Old Paul," had purchased his freedom after some forty years as a slave in South Carolina and Alabama, and had moved to New York to serve as a community leader of sorts there; among his belongings when he died were more than thirty texts (including Sayyid's) through which he had created a formal Muslim American curriculum for the benefit of this blossoming early American community (and the nation as a whole).

While these prominent and inspiring individuals (among others) helped contribute to the development of both the early Muslim American and American communities, another Revolutionary-era Muslim American community even more directly influenced the creation and laws of the new nation. The successes achieved by this South Carolina Muslim American community ironically led to its historical disappearance (at least in part), but not before it had definitely helped inspire one striking legal document and quite possibly influenced another even more crucial founding American principle.

The philosophical influence of Islam on Founding Fathers such as Thomas Jefferson has become well known in historical discussions of the founding era. Jefferson owned a copy of the Qur'an and wrote frequently about Islam in both his religious and political texts. For example, in the draft of his famous "Virginia Statute for Religious Freedom" (a direct predecessor to the U.S. Constitution's religious protections, on which more in a moment), Jefferson wrote that "neither Pagan nor Mahamedan [Muslim] nor Jew ought to be excluded from the civil rights of the Commonwealth because of his religion." Unfortunately, that sentence was struck from the statute before the Virginia General Assembly passed it in January 1786, but it clearly reflects Jefferson's inclusion of Islam and Muslim Americans in his religious and political philosophies. And such Founding-era Muslim Americans were not simply philosophical nor hypothetical, as illustrated most powerfully by the Charleston, South Carolina, Moroccan Muslim (or Moorish) American community.

The United States and Morocco shared a unique and important relationship in the Revolutionary and founding eras. The Sultanate of Morocco, under the rule of Sultan Mohammed ben Abdallah (Mohammed III), was the first country in the world to recognize the independent nation of the United States doing the American Revolution, doing so as early as a 1777 declaration that Moroccan ports were open to U.S. ships and commerce. Abdallah pursued a formal diplomatic relationship with the fledgling United States for much of the next decade, and in June 1786, the U.S. consul to France, Thomas Barclay, traveled to the Moroccan capital of Marrakesh to negotiate a treaty. He did so successfully, and the Treaty of Marrakesh, usually known as the Moroccan-American Treaty of Friendship, was signed by Thomas Jefferson and John Adams and then ratified by the Confederation Congress in July 1787 (and remains in operation to this day).

That Treaty of Friendship meant both that it was particularly easy for Moroccans to immigrate to the United States during this founding era and that Moroccan Americans already living in the United States enjoyed a somewhat unique and protected status. It's not entirely clear which category most contributed to the creation of the Free Moors of Charleston, South Carolina, a blossoming Moroccan Muslim (again, Moorish in the language of the era) American community in the period, but likely it was a combination of both. In the late 1780s and 1790s, North African nations were largely under the influence of the despotic figures known as the Barbary Pirates (and with whom the United States would fight a pair of early-nineteenth-century wars), and Moroccans thus had particular occasion to leave that region and immigrate to the United States. Yet as the individuals I've highlighted in this chapter illustrate, there were already many North Africans (and other Muslim Africans) living throughout the United States as slaves and former slaves. The community of Charleston Free Moors likely included members with experiences in both these originating categories.

The community members about whom we know the most are eight individuals—Francis, Daniel, Hammond, and Samuel, and their wives Fatima, Flora, Sarah, and Clarinda—who narrated their collective story as one of slavery and freedom: having become prisoners of war while fighting for their nation, they were sold into slavery and brought to South Carolina; over time, they purchased their freedom and began to form this Moroccan American community in Charleston. They told this story as part of a petition presented by the four men (on behalf of themselves and their wives) to the South Carolina House of Representatives on January 20, 1790. The petitioners sought to distinguish themselves from other African American residents of the state, who at the time (and until the Civil War) were subject to the discriminatory and exclusionary Negro Act of 1740 (which among other things made it illegal for enslaved African Americans to earn money and learn to write, and legal for slave owners to kill their slaves). The petitioners argued that, as both free-born subjects of a nation with which the United States had a treaty and Free Moors (rather than enslaved Africans) in their present state, they should be treated as citizens rather than Negroes under the state's laws.

The petition was referred to a House committee consisting of three particularly prominent representatives: Justice John Faucheraud Grimké (a judge and former Charleston mayor), General Charles Cotesworth Pinckney (a Revolutionary War veteran and Constitutional Convention delegate), and Edward Rutledge (the youngest signer of the Declaration of Independence and future South Carolina governor). Rutledge reported the committee's verdict to the full House of Representatives later in the same day, and it was entirely favorable to the petitioners. He wrote, "[The committee members] have Considered the same and are of opinion that no Law of this State can in its Construction or Operation apply to them, and that persons who were Subjects of the Emperor of Morocco being Free in this State are not triable by the Law for the better Ordering and Governing of Negroes and other Slaves." This decision, which came to be known as the Moors Sundry Act of 1790, operated with the force of law and was subsequently reported in both the *Charleston City Gazette* and the *Charleston State Gazette of South Carolina*.

That decision was a strikingly inclusive one, viewing these Moroccan Muslim Americans as (at least having the potential to be) full legal citizens of their adopted city and state. It did so, of course, in direct contrast to the state's continued exclusionary legal and social treatment of other African Americans (as part of but not limited to the system of chattel slavery). But for the members of this particular African American and Muslim American community, the decision opened up a wide range of possibilities of civic and communal life that would otherwise have been denied them: not only those outlawed under the Negro Act, such as earning money and traveling abroad; but also such opportunities as the right to vote, as serving on juries, and other guarantees of citizenship. As an ironic consequence of this decision and its effects, the members and especially the descendants of this Moroccan American community seem to have disappeared into the state's larger white population, and are much more difficult to trace in historical records as a result. But that in and of itself reflects the inclusive effects of this Muslim American community and its influential petition.

I would also argue for one other, more ambiguous but certainly possible and even more influential, effect of this founding-era Muslim American community. Along with Charles Cotesworth Pinckney, a second of South Carolina's four representatives to the Constitutional Convention was his cousin, Charles Pinckney. It was this latter Charles who drafted the only section in the Constitution that refers to religion in any way: Article VI, Clause 3, which reads, "but no religious test shall ever be required as a qualification to any office or public trust under the United States." This was a striking and impressively inclusive clause, as it contrasted the United States quite directly with most other Constitutional Republics (and nations) of the era: English law, for example, featured a number of connected Test Acts that excluded anyone not a member of the Church of England from holding public office; and most other European nations likewise featured a state religion to the practice which public officials had to belong (at least nominally). Yet through Pinckney's contribution to the Constitution, the new United States government would not only not do so, but would allow members of any religion (or no religion at all) to qualify for public office.

When Pinckney and his fellow Convention delegates brought the Constitution back to the state legislatures for the 1788–1789 ratification debates, legislators in South Carolina (as well as North Carolina) asked directly about this strikingly inclusive clause. In North Carolina, for example, the legislator Henry Abbot argued, "The exclusion of religious tests is by many thought dangerous and impolitic. They suppose that if there be no religious test required, pagans, deists, and Mahometans [Muslims] might obtain offices among us." And the Constitution's advocates replied precisely that yes, members of those communities might, and should have, the opportunity to do so: "It is objected that the people of America may, perhaps, choose representatives who have no religion at all, and that pagans and Mahometans may be admitted into offices. But how is it possible to exclude any set of men, without taking away that principle of religious freedom which we ourselves so warmly contend for?" I would contend that these arguments, like the Constitution's clause itself, were far from simply philosophical or political— that the existence of current Muslim American communities such as that in Charleston meant that the debate here was quite specifically over whether to include or exclude such Americans from the Constitution and its guaranteed rights. That they were included in this key clause reflects well on both the Constitution and the influence of this founding-era Moroccan Muslim American community.

Muslim Americans continued to contribute meaningfully to the United States throughout the nineteenth century. A number served in distinct ways during the Civil War, for example. Representative of the rank-and-file Muslim American soldier is Private Mohammed Kahn (also known as John Amma-hail), about whom we know primarily from his 1881 application for a pension from the 43rd New York Infantry Regiment; born in Persia (modern-day Iran), Kahn immigrated to the United States from Afghanistan in 1861 when he was about thirty years old, and enlisted just a couple months after his arrival. The highest-ranking Muslim American officer was Moses Osman (1822–1893), apparently a Pennsylvania native who was commissioned as a first lieutenant with the 104th Illinois Infantry and would be promoted to captain in September 1864. And perhaps the most unique Muslim American Civil War veteran was Mohammed Ali "Nicholas" Said, a Nigerian man who spent time as a slave to a Russian prince (Nicholas Vassilievitch Troubetz-koy, from whom Said received his "Christian" name) before gaining his freedom and coming to the United States in the antebellum era. He was teaching at an African American school in Detroit when the war broke out and eventually volunteered for the 55th Massachusetts Infantry Regiment, one of the first African American units. Said would publish *The Autobiography of Nicholas Said* in 1873, documenting the Civil War service and evolving mutlinational life story of this unique yet exemplary Muslim American.

While all of these and many other individuals highlight the continued presence and contribution of Muslim Americans throughout the century, it was at the turn of the twentieth century that Muslim American communities around the country truly began to develop in size and prominence. One such community were the arrivals from the region of the Ottoman Empire known as Syria (modern-day Lebanon), who immigrated to Ross, North Dakota, (among other places) in the first decade of the twentieth century. The first Syrian family to file a claim for a homestead near Ross did so in 1902, and many more followed in subsequent years. By 1929, the community was sizeable enough that it required a distinct and permanent place of worship, and so community members built a mosque, considered the oldest known structure built specifically to be a Muslim place of worship in the United States. The original structure was demolished in 1979, but in the early twenty-first century, a local Syrian American family raised money for a mosque/ memorial that now pays tribute to this groundbreaking Muslim American communal space.

While the Ross mosque holds that specific historical status as the nation's first built mosque, there were also other spaces both transformed and built to be mosques during the same period, each illustrating additional, evolving Muslim American communities. The Indian-born Ahmadiyya Muslim leader, Dr. Mufti Muhammad Sadiq, traveled to the United States in February 1920 on a mission to educate Americans about (and ideally convert some to) his particular Ahmadiyya strain of Islam, a global revivalist movement that had been founded in Punjab, India, in the last decade of the nineteenth century. Sadiq founded a Adhadiyya Muslim Community headquarters in Chicago, started the monthly magazine *The Muslim Sunrise* (which is still published today), and in 1922 commissioned the transformation of a building in the city's Bronzeville neighborhood into the Al-Sadiq Mosque (which is also still in operation). From this influential starting point the nation's Ahmadiyya Muslim community has continued to grow and now features four mosques in the Chicago area alone and more than forty throughout the United States.

The oldest built mosque still in operation was constructed just five years after Ross's and can be found in Cedar Rapids, Iowa. The Mother Mosque of America (also known as The Rose of Fraternity Lodge and the Moslem Temple) was likewise built by a community of Syrian (modern-day Lebanese) immigrants, with construction completed on February 15, 1934. Members of the Cedar Rapids Muslim American community also contributed to a number of other significant steps over the next couple of decades: in 1948 they constructed the first Muslim National Cemetery (which served as a burial site for Muslims from across the Midwest); in 1953 community member and World War II veteran Abdallah (sometimes Abdullah) Ingram convinced President Dwight D. Eisenhower to formally recognize Islam as an official religion within the U.S. military (meaning, among other effects, that Muslim American soldiers who passed away could be buried religiously rather than as "atheists"); and in 1952, Ingram and other leaders incorporated the International Muslim Society (IMS), which at its third annual meeting in 1954 was renamed the Federation of Islamic Associations of Canada and the United States (FIA). Ingram said, of his quest for military recognition, "I am fighting for my right, and the right of my people, to be recognized as a religious faith," and the same goal was pursued and achieved by this mid-twentieth-century Muslim American community as a whole.

These were but a few of the many significant early-twentieth-century Muslim American communities across the country, a list that would also have to include the Bosnian Muslims who, in 1906, founded Chicago's Džemijetul Hajrije (The Benevolent Society), the longest-standing incorporated Muslim American organization; the Polish Muslims who, in 1907,

founded New York City's first Muslim organization, the American Moham-
medan Society; and the Albanian Muslims who, in 1915, constructed a
mosque in Biddeford, Maine (the mosque no longer exists but the town still
features a Muslim American cemetery). Those additional examples reflect
even more clearly both the breadth of Muslim American national and ethnic
heritages and the geographic sweep across the United States of these groundbreaking and in many cases enduring communities.

Those communal identities and experiences continued to be complemented by striking individual stories, and no early-twentieth-century Muslim
American story (or American story period) is more striking than that of "Hot
Tamale Louie." Journalist and historian Kathryn Schulz covered the amazing
story of Louie and his many cultural and historical contexts in her June 6–13,
2016, *New Yorker* article "Citizen Khan"; Louie was the nickname of an
Afghani man named Zarif Khan, who immigrated to Sheridan, Wyoming, in
1909, and would, through his delicious tamales, go on to become one of the
town's most recognizable and beloved businessmen, patriarchs, and residents
before his tragic 1964 murder. Schulz's article is available in full online
(https://www.newyorker.com/magazine/2016/06/06/zarif-khans-tamales-
and-the-muslims-of-sheridan-wyoming), and deserves reading and response
on its own terms.

Here I'll highlight one particular part of Schulz's frame and Louie's
legacy. In late 2015, a handful of Muslim American families in Gillette,
Wyoming (ninety miles southeast of Sheridan), bought a one-story house and
converted it into a makeshift mosque. As so often in recent years, their
religious and civic efforts were opposed by exclusionary voices in the community, who began the "Stop Islam in Gillette" movement. Neither that
movement nor the Muslim community's more inclusive supporters seemed at
all aware of the region's longstanding Muslim American presence; while of
course a new community can and should still be welcomed and included, to
see Muslims as new to this part of Wyoming (or Wyoming at all) would be to
elide the story and history of Khan and the community he helped found.
Schulz concludes her article by examining the stakes of such collective memory or forgetting, in two paragraphs worth quoting in full:

> Who the Khans are and where they came from and what they're doing here is a
> long story, and a quintessentially American one. The history of immigrants is,
> to a huge extent, the history of this nation, though so is the pernicious practice
> of determining that some among us do not deserve full humanity, and full
> citizenship. Zarif Khan was deemed insufficiently American on the basis of
> skin color; ninety years later, when the presence of Muslims among us had
> come to seem like a crisis, his descendants were deemed insufficiently
> American on the basis of faith.
>
> Over and over, we forget what being American means. The radical prem-
> ise of our nation is that one people can be made from many, yet in each new

generation we find reasons to limit who those "many" can be—to wall off access to America, literally or figuratively. That impulse usually finds its roots in claims about who we used to be, but nativist nostalgia is a fantasy. We have always been a pluralist nation, with a past far richer and stranger than we choose to recall. Back when the streets of Sheridan were still dirt and Zarif Khan was still young, the Muslim who made his living selling Mexican food in the Wild West would put up a tamale for stakes and race local cowboys barefoot down Main Street. History does not record who won.

There are many such gaps or ambiguities in the histories of the Muslim American individuals and communities I've highlighted in this chapter, but those histories nonetheless all form part of that inclusive America for which Schulz argues so eloquently here—and have for as long as there's been an America of any kind.

There's one more side to Muslim American histories and communities that significantly contextualizes twenty-first-century exclusions and inclusions: the stories of Muslim refugees. Many Muslim arrivals and immigrants have come to the United States fleeing or escaping one historical and cultural violence or trauma or another, of course, but the official status of refugee also carries particular legal meanings and effects. The stories of a number of Muslim refugee populations from the last two decades exemplify this type of immigrant community, as well as their past and present contributions to American community and identity.

To highlight briefly a few of those refugee stories, the 1998 to 1999 Kosovo War, fought among numerous ethnic groups within the former Yugoslavia (and eventually featuring NATO air support and Albanian army ground forces), displaced more than a million Kosovar refugees, a significant percentage of whom were Muslim and 20,000 or so of whom came to the United States in 1999. Beginning in 2004, and for at least the next four years, more than 50 percent of the refugees admitted to the United States were Somali Muslims, fleeing the devastating civil war in that East African nation. Beginning in 2002, refugees from Myanmar (formerly Burma) to the United States were granted official refugee status for the first time; while that nation is predominantly Buddhist, many of its refugees are Muslims from the nation's Rohingya culture, fleeing religious and ethnic persecution.

In each of those cases, the arriving refugee communities have become vital elements of and contributors to twenty-first-century American society. Amy Slaughter, the COO of RefugePoint (which aided with the 1999 airlifts), notes of the Kosovar refugees, the process "was life-saving for those refugees who came to the U.S., made positive contributions to the U.S. society and economy, and benefited the rebuilding of Kosovo with remittances and return of talent and assets." Arthur Nazaryan, a Somali American photojournalist, says of his project featuring the Somali community in Minnesota (which numbers more than 150,000, the largest in any American state), "Ultimately, I hope these photos will demonstrate that the typical Somali is no less American than any other Minnesotan." And many of the 13,000 Myanmar Rohingya refugees to the United States since 2002 have settled in Chicago, founding (among many other community achievements) the Rohingya Cultural Center that offers a model of communal support and civic life for this refugee community and others like it.

The Syrian refugees on whom many of the exclusionary, Islamophobic narratives of the last few years have focused have their own specific national and historical contexts and stories, as does each of those prior communities of course. Yet they also form part of this longstanding and ongoing story of Muslim refugees to the United States, a history that complements but also extends and amplifies the overall story, presence, and contributions of Muslim Americans. There is nothing new about twenty-first-century Muslim Americans, nor do these contemporary Muslim arrivals and existing communities represent identities outside of or hostile to American identity overall. Instead, in every sense and on every level, Muslim Americans have been a foundational and integral part of the United States throughout its history. No inclusive vision of the nation, then and now, would be complete without them.

Conclusion

The Battle in the Age of Trump

The exclusionary, white supremacist definition of American identity has undergone a dramatic resurgence in recent years. As I trace in chapter 8, the Islamophobic exclusions that took center stage after the September 11, 2001, terrorist attacks constituted one specific and potent part of that resurgence. But the two decades since have also seen the rise of a much broader and more overarching exclusionary narrative of American identity, one succinctly illustrated by the xenophobic and exclusionary images of and responses to the candidacy and presidency of Barack Obama.

The Muslim conspiracy theories I highlighted in chapter 8 were part of that trend, as were the complementary, if even broader, "Birther" conspiracy theories about Obama's alleged Kenyan nativity. Those Birther theories influenced GOP voters in particular in striking and ongoing ways; as recently as a December 2017 YouGov survey, 51 percent of registered Republicans continue to believe Obama to have been born in Kenya (and 57 percent of 2016 Trump voters in the same poll believe it, which is no surprise considering Trump was the most prominent and vocal Birther for a number of years). But even for those less partisan and more rational Americans who didn't adhere in any way to Birtherism, certain features of Obama's identity—his father's status as a Kenyan immigrant, his years living in Indonesia when his mother married an Indonesian man, perhaps even his name—seemed to suggest something foreign to American identity. Illustrating this perspective was an October 20, 2008, *Time* magazine cover story (by Peter Beinart) entitled, "Is Barack Obama American Enough?"

Beinart begins his story by quoting vice presidential nominee Sarah Palin, who remarked in an October 6 campaign rally, "I am just so fearful that this is not a man who sees America the way that you and I see America." But in the course of the article Beinart's analyses go well beyond both this overtly partisan and campaign rhetoric and the question of perspective or worldview, and enter instead into debates over both Obama's identity and American identity. While Beinart in no way endorses narratives of Obama as non- or anti-American, neither does he refute them; instead, the story presents those exclusionary narratives as one of a few competing visions of this particular candidate and, though him, of the collective identity of the nation he was campaigning to lead. Of course Beinart and *Time* did not invent those exclusionary narratives nor that debate, but their presence at the heart of a cover story in this prominent, well-respected news magazine reflects just how potent they had already become by October 2008.

Obama won the presidency in November 2008, but that campaign debate foreshadowed one of the most consistent opposition responses to his presidency, a narrative that went far beyond political or partisan arguments about his administration or policies and far into exclusionary images of both Obama and America. This narrative was exemplified by one of the chief rallying cries of the anti-Obama forces, a slogan that emerged as early as the summer of 2009 and would endure throughout Obama's two terms as president: "I want my country back!" Journalist Wade Clark Roof was one of the first to analyze that phrase at length, in his October 1, 2009, *Religion Dispatches* piece entitled, "'I Want My Country Back!': The Demography of Discontent." As Roof notes, the phrase stemmed from a number of factors, including the economy and specifically the ongoing effects of the 2008 recession. Yet in his final paragraph, he makes the vital connection that such economic anxieties have "combined with symbolic loss of identity and privilege as an older Anglo-Protestant culture . . . to explain what is going on."

I would agree, and would moreover argue that through that symbolic, cultural layer the phrase exemplifies an exclusionary narrative of America, on two key and interconnected levels: "my country," which suggests directly a vision of national identity; and "back," which indicates that this America has been threatened or taken, presumably by some "they" not part of the "we" to which this speaker belongs. Although that national "we" is not in the phrase itself overtly defined as "Anglo-Protestant culture" or some other exclusionary and white supremacist vision, it is no coincidence that the phrase emerged from voices and communities entirely opposed to the presidency of the man who (from their perspective) might not have been born in the country, might be a secret Muslim, and in any case was simply not "American enough." In this narrative, Barack Obama represented and even embodied the "they" who had taken the country, and it was first and foremost the exclusionary images of his nationality, heritage, race and ethnicity, religion, and his very identity that comprised the core of that foreign and threatening presence.

As foreshadowed by his 2010–2011 rise to political prominence as the Birther-in-Chief, Donald Trump's 2016 presidential campaign built upon and amplified this exclusionary narrative of Obama and America. Trump's campaign slogan, "Make America Great Again!," is even more superficially (and purposefully) ambiguous than "I want my country back!"—how that prior national greatness is defined is open to interpretation, and could in theory allow for any number of different perspectives and communities to embrace it. But in his June 16, 2015, campaign launching speech, much of which was dedicated to communicating that slogan for the first time, Trump tellingly began with a much more specific and exclusionary perspective:

> The U.S. has become a dumping ground for everybody else's problems. . . . When Mexico sends its people, they're not sending their best. They're not sending you. They're not sending you. They're sending people that have lots of problems, and they're bringing those problems with [them]. They're bringing drugs. They're bringing crime. They're rapists. And some, I assume, are good people. . . . It's coming from more than Mexico. It's coming from all over South and Latin America, and it's coming probably from the Middle East. But we don't know. Because we have no protection and we have no competence, we don't know what's happening. And it's got to stop and it's got to stop fast.

Responding to this origin point, and building upon centuries of exclusionary histories and narratives, the #MAGA community has consistently and thoroughly latched onto this particular side to the slogan and the Trump era. Illustrating the multiple layers to that exclusionary perspective is Linda Dwire, a Colorado woman captured on an October 2018 viral video berating both two Spanish-speaking customers and a white ally of theirs at a grocery store. Dwire first attacked the two women, arguing, "You're in America. You're in my country. You can't speak Spanish here." She amplified this perspective in subsequent interviews, claiming immigrants would "rather have their country here. I don't mind them coming as long as they want to be an American." And when another white woman, Kamira Trent, confronted Dwire and asked her to stop harassing the two customers, Dwire responded, "You come from a generation that's destroying this country. . . . You will lose your country. You know what, you will lose this country." This perspective directly weds an exclusionary vision of language, culture, and immigration to fears of "losing" the country, against which contrasting goals of taking the country back and making it great again are implied but clear.

While Trump's campaign and presidency have served as inspirations and focal points for many of these exclusionary narratives and voices, the last few years have likewise featured a more multifaceted and overarching resurgence of exclusionary, white supremacist voices. These exclusionary narratives, both Trump-centered and otherwise, have emerged in response to a number of contemporary issues and conversations, many tied directly to the kinds of topics and histories through which I've moved in this book's chapters.

Anti-immigrant and anti-Muslim exclusions have been two of the most central threads, and often have been directly linked to one another, as Trump did in that campaign launching speech and has returned to in October 2018 with his assertions that there are "Middle East" elements within the so-called migrant caravan making its way through Central America and Mexico. It's even more telling that one of the first postinauguration policy proposals advanced by the Trump administration, and the one for which they have fought most consistently despite frequent legal setbacks, was the travel or Muslim ban, an exclusionary immigration law that focuses directly on Muslim-majority nations (but that in the currently existing 3.0 iteration also includes Venezuelan government officials, wedding that Islamophobia to an almost random but illustrative Hispanic exclusion as well). The exclusionary fears directed at Syrian refugees (and the menacing "Sharia law" that they would bring with them) have offered one more layer to these anti-immigrant and anti-Muslim narratives.

The Trump administration has also floated or proposed a number of other anti-immigrant policies, many of which echo the Chinese Exclusion Act era and its aftermaths quite closely. A focus of those proposals has been the elimination of family reunification policies (known in this exclusionary narrative as "chain migration"), a change that would serve at least as much to affect and damage existing American families and communities as potential new arrivals. The administration has also threatened to strip the citizenship and legal status from various categories of immigrants, attacks on the legal and civic identities of these communities that parallel not only Chinese exclusion but also the twentieth century's exclusionary treatments of both Filipino and Japanese Americans. And the constant raids, crackdowns, and detention centers run by the Immigration and Customs Enforcement agency (ICE), exemplified with particularly destructive force by the detentions and family separations of Hispanic American arrivals at the Mexican border, echo the detentions of Chinese arrivals at Angel Island and Japanese internees in the camps, among other exclusionary histories and settings.

While those family detentions and separations at the border have comprised a particularly visible and extreme unfolding exclusion, anti-Mexican and anti-Hispanic exclusions have been a defining element of the last few years in even broader and more telling ways. Perhaps the most divisive and ugly of those exclusions has been the use of "Build the wall!" chants as a taunt and attack directed at Mexican and Hispanic individuals and communities in a variety of settings. No single moment summed up that exclusionary trend more succinctly than the "Build the wall!" chants directed by seventh-graders at some of their Hispanic classmates at Michigan's Royal Oak Middle School the day after Trump's election; clearly and tragically, these impressionable young people had taken Trump's victory (and, one assumes, their parents' attitudes) as an impetus to wed bullying (a longstanding and evolving American problem of its own) to exclusion. A week later, a noose was found in a boys' bathroom at the school, offering another striking echo of historical exclusions and an extension of them into these contemporary, all-too-present divisions and discriminations.

Whatever the particular meanings of that middle school noose, the larger histories it echoes are all too clear, and indeed exclusionary, white supremacist attitudes toward African Americans have likewise potently reemerged over the last few years. The most overt and violent such exclusionary narrative was voiced by Dylann Roof, the neo-Nazi murderer of nine African American parishioners at Charleston, South Carolina's historic Emanuel African Methodist Episcopal Church in June 2015. Before he opened fire, Roof apparently told his victims, "You rape our women, and you're taking over our country, and you have to go." Two years later, the neo-Nazis and white supremacists who rallied in Charlottesville, Virginia, likewise wed racist attitudes toward African American histories and communities (centered around their defense of the city's controversial Confederate memorials) to broader exclusionary narratives, as illustrated by their chants of "Jews will not replace us!" as they marched through the city. And in March 2018, Trump renewed his frequent attacks on African American NFL players protesting injustice and police brutality with a particularly exclusionary sentiment: "You have to stand proudly for the national anthem, or you shouldn't be there. Maybe you shouldn't be in the country."

Native Americans have not been exempt from these twenty-first-century exclusions either. The illegal incursion of the Dakota Access Pipeline (DAPL) onto sovereign and sacred Sioux land on North Dakota's Standing Rock Reservation in early 2016, a corporate invasion supported by governmental and official voices from Trump himself down to local law enforcement agencies, echoed all too closely the policies and narratives behind nineteenth-century Indian Removal. Over the same period, North Dakota's state legislature passed a restrictive and exclusionary voter ID law, one that by requiring voters to have a residential address overtly and purposefully disenfranchised most of the state's Native American voters (since most of those living on reservations have P.O. boxes instead). In October 2018, the Supreme Court upheld that exclusionary law as constitutional (at least for the purposes of the upcoming midterm elections), adding one more layer to the official and governmental support for such attempted exclusions of Native Americans from American civic life and collective identity.

Alongside and amplifying all those exclusionary narratives and policies has been the Trump era's most violent and horrific trend: white supremacist

hate crimes targeting Americans of color and featuring consistently exclusionary rhetoric and motivations. I wrote in the introduction about one such
exclusionary hate crime, the May 2017 Portland, Oregon, harassment of two
teenage girls (one Muslim and one African American) and stabbing of three
white allies by white supremacist Jeremy Christian; Christian's accompanying statements, such as "You call it terrorism, I call it patriotism," illustrate
his exclusionary vision of America quite clearly. Among the numerous other
such hate crimes over the last couple years, the frequent attacks on Sikh
Americans (anti-Sikh violence has risen nearly 20 percent since the 2016
election) have exemplified these exclusionary narratives, as illustrated by the
July 2018, ironic and brutal attack on Turlock, California's Surjit Malhi;
Malhi, a staunch local Republican, was erecting lawn signs in support of
GOP congressman Jeff Denham when two white supremacists accosted and
beat him savagely, shouting "Go back to your country" and spray painting a
Celtic cross (a white supremacist and neo-Nazi symbol) on his pickup truck.
To quote Valarie Kaur, a lawyer and Sikh activist from Los Angeles whose
words apply to all of these contemporary exclusions, "The current surge is
the most dangerous we have seen, because it is fueled by an administration
that has mainstreamed profiling and bigotry in words and actions."

So in the face of such an administration, such exclusionary violence and
narratives, such a fraught and divisive historical moment, how should those
of us who would advocate for an alternative, inclusive vision of America
respond? One clear and understandable answer is to highlight the long history of exclusions, to contextualize our current moment as part of that foundational, longstanding, and ongoing exclusionary definition of American identity. It's this emphasis on exclusionary national histories, for example, that
led to the clever and compelling phrase, "America Was Never Great," a
direct response to Trump's slogan first popularized by a young African
American woman (twenty-two-year-old Staten Island Home Depot employee
Krystal Lake) wearing it on a hat of her own.

I believe there are significant limits to that phrase and perspective, however. For one thing, it more or less thoroughly surrenders in the battle to
define America, ceding all definitions of our national community and identity to the exclusionary voices and vision. I argued in my last book, *History
and Hope in American Literature: Models of Critical Patriotism* (2016),
against ceding the concept of patriotism to simplifying and celebratory versions, and I would say the same about definitions of America: we can't allow
white supremacist definitions of the nation to go uncontested. And for another, even more important thing, "America Was Never Great" makes it
seem as if the exclusionary histories have been the whole or at least the
principal story, as if those exclusions have comprised the central thread of
America's identity and story.

Of course exclusionary histories and visions of the nation have been one such central thread, present and prominent across every American time period and culture, as the opening of each of my chapters has illustrated. But what those chapters as a whole have argued is that exclusionary narratives and definitions have consistently, indeed constantly, been contrasted and challenged by inclusive alternatives, opposing visions and forces in a battle to define American identity and community. As the remainder of each chapter has argued at length, those inclusive alternatives have likewise been present in every historical moment and for every American community, responding to and resisting exclusion and imagining and modeling an inclusive America that features all these cultures and histories, voices and stories, identities and futures.

Those inclusive figures and stories are what have made America great, constitute an ideal and even exceptional national identity of which we have all too often fallen short but which they offer as a continued example and beacon. Nothing is more important in the age of Trump than carrying forward the fight to remember, celebrate, be inspired by, and learn from these inclusive models as we move forward. The battle to define who is an American has never been more heated nor more relevant, and despite the resurgent exclusionary presence and potency, we the people can and must still be an inclusive national community.

A Note on Sources

INTRODUCTION: THE BATTLE
OVER WHO IS AN AMERICAN

A number of excellent recent public scholarly books have traced America's exclusionary histories: Nell Irvin Painter, *The History of White People* (New York: W.W. Norton, 2011); Kevin Kruse, *One Nation Under God: How Corporate America Invented Christian America* (New York: Basic Books, 2015); Ibram X. Kendi, *Stamped from the Beginning: The Definitive History of Racist Ideas in America* (New York: Nation Books, 2016); Richard T. Hughes, *Myths America Lives By: White Supremacy and the Stories That Give Us Meaning* (Urbana: University of Illinois Press, 2018, 2nd edition); and Jill Lepore, *These Truths: A History of the United States* (New York: W.W. Norton, 2018). For an analysis of exclusion and inclusion in urban spaces, see Tobias Armborst, *The Arsenal of Exclusion & Inclusion* (New York: Actar Publishers, 2017); for one focused on literature, see Josh Toth, *Stranger America: A Narrative Ethics of Exclusion* (Charlottesville: University of Virginia Press, 2018).

For exemplary analyses of these threads in the histories of immigration, ethnicity and race, and culture, see Roger Daniels, *Coming to America: A History of Immigration and Ethnicity in American Life* (New York: Harper Books, 2002); Paul Spickard, *Almost All Aliens: Immigration, Race, and Colonialism in American History and Identity* (New York: Routledge, 2007); Greg Carter, *The United States of the United Races: A Utopian History of Racial Mixing* (New York: New York University Press, 2013); and Shannon Latkin Anderson, *Immigration, Assimilation, and the Cultural Construction of American National Identity* (New York: Routledge, 2016). For a relevant analysis of de Crèvecoeur, see Katy Chiles, *Transformable Race: Surprising*

Metamorphoses in the Literature of Early America (New York: Oxford University Press, 2014). For recent Ida B. Wells scholarship, see Kristina DuRocher, *Ida B. Wells: Social Reformer and Activist* (New York: Routledge, 2017); and *Political Pioneer of the Press: Ida B. Wells-Barnett and Her Transnational Crusade for Social Justice*, edited by Lori Amber Roessner and Jodi Rightler-McDaniels (Lanham, MD: Lexington Books, 2018).

CHAPTER 1: CONQUISTADORS AND CROSS-CULTURAL COMMUNITIES

For three exemplary recent analyses of Christopher Columbus and his contexts, see Evelina Gužauskytė, *Christopher Columbus's Naming in the Diarios of the Four Voyages (1492–1504): A Discourse of Negotiation* (Toronto: University of Toronto Press, 2014); Elise Bartosik-Velez, *The Legacy of Christopher Columbus in the Americas: New Nations and a Transatlantic Discourse of Empire* (Nashville, TN: Vanderbilt University Press, 2014); and Elizabeth M. Willingham, *The Mythical Indies and Columbus's Apocalyptic Letter: Imagining the Americas in the Late Middle Ages* (Brighton, UK: Sussex Academic Press, 2016). For primary sources, see James E. Wadsworth, ed., *Columbus and His First Voyage: A History in Documents* (London: Bloomsbury Press, 2016). For broader analyses of the Americas postcontact, see Nicolás Wey Gómez, *The Tropics of Empire: Why Columbus Sailed South to the Indies* (Cambridge, MA: MIT Press, 2008); Fabienne Viala, *The Post-Columbus Syndrome: Identities, Cultural Nationalism, and Commemorations in the Caribbean* (New York: Palgrave Macmillan, 2014); Anna Brickhouse, *The Unsettlement of America: Translation, Interpretation, and the Story of Don Luis de Velasco, 1560–1945* (Oxford: Oxford University Press, 2015); and *Caribbean Globalizations, 1492 to the Present Day*, edited by Eva Sansavior and Richard Scholar (Liverpool: Liverpool University Press, 2015).

For recent works on las Casas, see Daniel Castro, *Another Face of Empire: Bartolomé de las Casas, Indigenous Rights, and Ecclesiastical Imperialism* (Durham, NC: Duke University Press, 2007); Lawrence A. Clayton, *Bartolomé de las Casas and the Conquest of the Americas* (Malden, MA: Wiley-Blackwell, 2011); Lawrence A. Clayton, *Bartolomé de las Casas: A Biography* (New York: Cambridge University Press, 2012); and David Thomas Orique, *To Heaven or to Hell: Bartolomé de las Casas's Confesionario* (University Park: Pennsylvania State University Press, 2018). For de Vaca, see M. Carmen Gómez-Galisteo, *Early Visions and Representations of America: Alvar Nuñez Cabeza de Vaca's Naufragios and William Bradford's Of Plymouth Plantation* (New York: Bloomsbury Books, 2013); William K. Hartmann, *Searching for Golden Empires: Epic Cultural Collisions in Six-*

teenth-Century America (Tucson: University of Arizona Press, 2014); Robin Varnum, *Alvar Nuñez Cabeza de Vaca: American Trailblazer* (Norman: University of Oklahoma Press, 2014); and Alvar Nuñez Cabeza de Vaca, *Chronicle of the Narváez Expedition: A New Translation, Context, Criticism* (New York: W.W. Norton, 2013). For an alternate reading of de Vaca's journey, see Dennis F. Herrick, *Esteban: The African Slave Who Explored America* (Albuquerque: University of New Mexico Press, 2018).

For analyses of Native Americans and the Pilgrims, see David Read, *New World, Known World: Shaping Knowledge in Early American Writing* (Columbia: University of Missouri Press, 2005); Nathaniel Philbrick, *Mayflower: A Story of Courage, Community, and War* (New York: Viking Books, 2006); Cynthia Van Zandt, *Brothers Among Nations: The Pursuit of Intercultural Alliances in Early America, 1580–1660* (New York: Oxford University Press, 2008); Betty Booth Donahue, *Bradford's Indian Book: Being the True Roote & Rise of American Letters as Revealed by the Native Text Embedded in* Of Plimoth Plantation (Gainesville: University Press of Florida, 2011); and Gómez-Galisteo. For Native Americans after contact, including Tisquantum and the Wampanoag, see Pauline Turner Strong, *Captive Selves, Captivating Others: The Politics and Poetics of Colonial American Captivity Narratives* (Boulder, CO: Westview Press, 1999); *Early Native Literacies in New England: A Documentary and Critical Anthology*, edited by Kristina Bross and Hilary E. Wyss (Amherst: University of Massachusetts Press, 2008); *Dawnland Voices: An Anthology of Indigenous Writing from New England* (Lincoln: University of Nebraska Press, 2014); and Lisa Brooks, *Our Beloved Kin: A New History of King Philip's War* (New Haven: Yale University Press, 2018).

CHAPTER 2: SLAVES, REVOLUTIONARY ENEMIES OR EXEMPLARS

For two particularly strong recent takes on this chapter's histories, see Michael F. Conlin, *One Nation Divided by Slavery: Remembering the American Revolution while Marching toward the Civil War* (Kent, OH: Kent State University Press, 2015); and Russell Shorto, *Revolution Song: A Story of American Freedom* (New York: W.W. Norton, 2018). For analyses of race and the nation's founding, see Edmund Morgan, *American Slavery, American Freedom: The Ordeal of Colonial Virginia* (New York: W.W. Norton, 1975); Ari Helo, *Thomas Jefferson's Ethics and the Politics of Human Progress: The Morality of a Slaveholder* (New York: Cambridge University Press, 2014); Paul Finkelman, *Slavery and the Founders: Race and Liberty in the Age of Jefferson* (Armonk, NY: M.E. Sharpe, 2014); Ibram X. Kendi; Padraig Riley, *Slavery and the Democratic Conscience: Political Life in Jeffersonian America* (Philadelphia: University of Pennsylvania Press, 2016); and Sean Wilentz, *No Property in Man: Slavery and Antislavery at the Nation's Founding* (Cambridge, MA: Harvard University Press, 2018). For African Americans and the Revolution, see Robert Ewell Greene, *Black Courage, 1775–1783: Documentation of Black Participation in the American Revolution* (Washington: National Society of the Daughters of the American Revolution, 1984); Glenn A. Knoblock, *"Strong and Brave Fellows": New Hampshire's Black Soldiers and Sailors of the American Revolution, 1775– 1784* (Jefferson, NC: McFarland, 2003); Joyce Lee Malcolm, *Peter's War: A New England Slave Boy and the American Revolution* (New Haven, CT: Yale University Press, 2009); Douglas Egerton, *Death or Liberty: African Americans and Revolutionary America* (New York: Oxford University Press, 2009); Alan Gilbert, *Black Patriots and Loyalists: Fighting for Emancipation in the War for Independence* (Chicago: University of Chicago Press, 2012); and Judith Van Buskirk, *Standing in Their Own Light: African American Patriots in the American Revolution* (Norman: University of Oklahoma Press, 2017).

For more on Attucks, see Neil Longley York, *The Boston Massacre: A History with Documents* (New York: Routledge, 2010) and Mitchell A. Kachun, *First Martyr of Liberty: Crispus Attucks in American Memory* (New York: Oxford University Press, 2017). For Wheatley, see Vincent Carretta, *Phillis Wheatley: Biography of a Genius in Bondage* (Athens, GA: University of Georgia Press, 2011); G. J. Barker-Benfield, *Phillis Wheatley Chooses Freedom: History, Poetry, and the Ideals of the American Revolution* (New York: New York University Press, 2018). The two best works on Elizabeth Freeman are geared toward young adults: Ben Z. Rose, *Mother of Freedom: Mum Bett and the Roots of Abolition* (Waverly, MA: TreeLine Press, 2009); and Jana Laiz, *A Free Woman on God's Earth: The True Story of Elizabeth "Mumbet" Freeman, the Slave Who Won her Freedom* (Berkshires, MA: Crow Flies Press, 2009). See also Robert P. Green Jr., ed., *Equal Protection and the African American Constitutional Experience: A Documentary History* (Westport, CT: Greenwood Press, 2000).

CHAPTER 3: INDIAN REMOVAL
AND INSPIRING RESISTANCE

For overall take on Native Americans and definitions of American identity, see David L. Moore, *That Dream Shall Have a Name: Native Americans Rewriting America* (Lincoln: University of Nebraska Press, 2014); David Carlson, *Imagining Sovereignty: Self-Determination in American Indian Law and Literature* (Norman: University of Oklahoma Press, 2016); and Alan Parker, *Pathways to Indigenous Nation Sovereignty: A Chronicle of Federal*

Policy Developments (East Lansing, MI: Makwa Enewed, 2018). For more on Indian Removal, see Jason Edward Black, *American Indians and the Rhetoric of Removal and Allotment* (Jackson: University Press of Mississippi, 2015); William W. Winn, *The Triumph of the Ecunnau-Nuxulgee: Land Speculators, George M. Troup, State Rights, and the Removal of the Creek Indians from Georgia and Alabama, 1825–38* (Macon, GA: Mercer University Press, 2015); Christopher Haveman, *Rivers of Sand: Creek Indian Emigration, Relocation, and Ethnic Cleansing in the American South* (Lincoln: University of Nebraska Press, 2016); *Bending Their Way Onward: Creek Indian Removal in Documents*, edited by Haveman (Lincoln: University of Nebraska Press, 2017); Theda Perdue, *The Cherokee Removal: A Brief History with Documents* (Boston, MA: Bedford/St. Martin's, 2016); Alfred A. Cave, *Sharp Knife: Andrew Jackson and the American Indians* (Santa Barbara, CA: Praeger, 2017); and Andrew Denson, *Monuments to Absence: Cherokee Removal and the Contest over Southern Memory* (Chapel Hill: University of North Carolina Press, 2017).

For Cherokee responses to Removal, see Daniel Blake Smith, *An American Betrayal: Cherokee Patriots and the Trail of Tears* (New York: Henry Holt, 2011); Joshua B. Nelson, *Progressive Traditions: Identity in Cherokee Literature and Culture* (Norman, OK: University of Oklahoma Press, 2014); Gregory D. Smithers, *The Cherokee Diaspora: An Indigenous History of Migration, Resettlement, and Identity* (New Haven, CT: Yale University Press, 2015); Julie L. Reed, *Serving the Nation: Cherokee Sovereignty and Social Welfare, 1800–1907* (Norman: University of Oklahoma Press, 2016); and Dan B. Wimberly, *Cherokee in Controversy: The Life of Jesse Bushyhead* (Macon, GA: Mercer University Press, 2017). For the Mashpee Revolt, see Daniel R. Mandell, *Tribe, Race, History: Native Americans in Southern New England, 1780–1880* (Baltimore: Johns Hopkins University Press, 2008); and Sandra M. Gustafson, *Imagining Deliberative Democracy in the Early American Republic* (Chicago: University of Chicago Press, 2011). For Apess, see, *On Our Own Ground: The Complete Writings of William Apess, a Pequot*, edited by Barry O'Connell (Amherst: University of Massachusetts Press, 1992); Philip F. Gura, *The Life of William Apess, Pequot* (Chapel Hill: University of North Carolina Press, 2014); and Drew Lopenzina. *Through an Indian's Looking-Glass: A Cultural Biography of William Apess, Pequot* (Amhert: University of Massachusetts Press, 2017).

CHAPTER 4: MEXICAN AMERICANS HAVE NEVER LEFT

For recent histories of the Mexican-American War, see Hunt Janin, *The California Campaigns of the U.S.-Mexican War, 1846–1848* (Jefferson, NC: McFarland, 2015); Nathan A. Jennings, *Riding for the Lone Star: Frontier*

Cavalry and the Texas Way of War, 1822–1865 (Denton, TX: University of North Texas Press, 2016); Andrea Ferraris, *The Battle of Churubusco: American Rebels in the Mexican-American War* (Seattle: Fantagraphics Books, 2017); Peter Guardino, *The Dead March: A History of the Mexican-American War* (Cambridge, MA: Harvard University Press, 2017); John M. Belohlavek, *Patriots, Prostitutes, and Spies: Women and the Mexican-American War* (Charlottesville: University of Virginia Press, 2017). For relevant histories of Mexican American communities after the war, see William S. Kiser, *Turmoil on the Rio Grande: History of the Mesilla Valley, 1846–1865* (College Station: Texas A&M University Press, 2011); Tamara Venit Shelton, *A Squatter's Republic: Land and the Politics of Monopoly in California, 1850–1900* (Berkeley: University of California Press, 2013); Steven Bender, *How the West Was Juan: Reimagining the U.S.-Mexico Border* (San Diego: San Diego State University Press, 2017); and James David Nichols, *The Limits of Liberty: Mobility and the Making of the Eastern U.S.-Mexico Border* (Lincoln: University of Nebraska Press, 2018).

For overall Mexican American histories, see Neil Foley, *Mexicans in the Making of America* (Cambridge, MA: Harvard University Press, 2014); Carey McWilliams, *North from Mexico: The Spanish-Speaking People of the United States* (Santa Barbara, CA: Praeger, 2016, 3rd edition); Felipe Gonzales, *Política: Nuevomexicanos and American Political Incorporation, 1821–1910* (Lincoln: University of Nebraska Press, 2016); and Zaragosa Vargas, *Crucible of Struggle: A History of Mexican Americans from Colonial Times to the Present Era* (New York: Oxford University Press, 2017, 2nd edition). For Tejanos, see Charles H. Harris, *The Plan de San Diego: Tejano Rebellion, Mexican Intrigue* (Lincoln: University of Nebraska Press, 2013); Antonio Menchaca, *Recollections of a Tejano Life: Antonio Menchaca in Texas History*, edited by Timothy Matovina and Jesús F. de la Teja (Austin: University of Texas Press, 2013); Arnoldo De León, *Tejano West Texas* (College Station: Texas A&M University Press, 2015); Jerry D. Thompson, *Tejano Tiger: José de los Santos Benavides and the Texas-Mexico Borderlands, 1823–1891* (Fort Worth, TX: TCU Press, 2017). For San Diego, see Matthew F. Bokovoy, *The San Diego World's Fairs and Southwestern Memory, 1880–1940* (Albuquerque: University of New Mexico Press, 2005); *Chicano San Diego: Cultural Space and the Struggle for Justice*, edited by Richard Griswold del Castillo (Tucson: University of Arizona Press, 2007); and Rudy Guevarra, *Becoming Mexipino: Multiethnic Identities and Communities in San Diego* (New Brunswick, NJ: Rutgers University Press, 2012).

For Ruiz de Burton, see *Conflicts of Interest: The Letters of Maria Amparo Ruiz de Burton*, edited by Rosaura Sánchez and Beatrice Pita (Houston: Arte Público Press, 2001); *Maria Amparo Ruiz de Burton: Critical and Pedagogical Perspectives*, edited by Amelia María de la Luz Montes and Anne Elizabeth Goldman (Lincoln: University of Nebraska Press, 2004); John-

Michael Rivera, *The Emergence of Mexican America: Recovering Stories of Mexican Peoplehood in U.S. Culture* (New York: New York University Press, 2006); Vincent Pérez, *Remembering the Hacienda: History and Memory in the Mexican American Southwest* (College Station: Texas A&M University Press, 2006); and Karen R. Roybal, *Archives of Dispossession: Recovering the Testimonios of Mexican American Herederas, 1848–1960* (Chapel Hill: University of North Carolina Press, 2017). For Mena, see *"The only efficient instrument": American Women Writers and the Periodical, 1837–1916*, edited by Aleta Feinsod Cane and Susan Alves (Iowa City: University of Iowa City Press, 2001); and Dora Alicia Ramírez, *Medical Imagery and Fragmentation: Modernism, Scientific Discourse, and the Mexican/Indigenous Body, 1870–1940s* (Lanham, MD: Lexington Books, 2017). For Mexican American civil rights, see Cynthia Orozco, *No Mexicans, Women, or Dogs Allowed: The Rise of the Mexican American Civil Rights Movement* (Austin: University of Texas Press, 2009); Carlos Kevin Blanton, *George I. Sánchez: The Long Fight for Mexican American Integration* (New Haven: Yale University Press, 2014); Anthony Quiroz, *Leaders of the Mexican American Generation: Biographical Essays* (Boulder, CO: University Press of Colorado, 2014); and Richard J. Gonzales, *Raza Rising: Chicanos in North Texas* (Denton, TX: University of North Texas Press, 2016).

CHAPTER 5: UN-AMERICAN AND UNSUCCESSFUL CHINESE EXCLUSIONS

For histories of Chinese Exclusion, see Ben Railton, *The Chinese Exclusion Act: What It Can Teach Us about America* (New York: Palgrave Macmillan, 2013); Liping Zhu, *The Road to Chinese Exclusion: The Denver Riot, 1880 Election, and the Rise of the West* (Lawrence: University Press of Kansas, 2013); John Kuo Wei Tchen, *Chinese American: Exclusion/Inclusion* (London: Scale Arts & Heritage, 2014); David Atkinson, *The Burden of White Supremacy: Containing Asian Migration in the British Empire and the United States* (Chapel Hill: University of North Carolina Press, 2016); Lon Kurashige, *Two Faces of Exclusion: The Untold History of Anti-Asian Racism in the United States* (Chapel Hill: University of North Carolina Press, 2016); and Beth Lew-Williams, *The Chinese Must Go: Violence, Exclusion, and the Making of the Alien in America* (Cambridge, MA: Harvard University Press, 2018). For connections to immigration law, see David FitzGerald, *Culling the Masses: The Democratic Origins of Racist Immigration Policy in the Americas* (Cambridge, MA: Harvard University Press, 2014); Kunal Madhukar Parker, *Making Foreigners: Immigration and Citizenship Law in America, 1600–2000* (New York: Cambridge University Press, 2015); Hidetaka Hirota, *Expelling the Poor: Atlantic Seaboard States and the Nine-*

teenth-Century Origins of American Immigration Policy (New York: Oxford University Press, 2017); and *Immigration and the Law: Race, Citizenship, and Social Control*, edited by Sofía Espinoza Álvarez and Martin Guevara Urbina (Tucson: University of Arizona Press, 2018).

For Chinese American histories, see H. Mark Lai, *Becoming Chinese American: A History of Communities and Institutions* (Walnut Creek, CA: AltaMira, 2004); *Island: Poetry and History of Chinese Immigrants on Angel Island, 1910–1940*, edited by Him Mark Lai, Genny Lim, and Judy Yung (Seattle: University of Washington Press, 2014, 2nd edition); Shelly Sang-Hee Lee, *A New History of Asian America* (New York: Routledge, 2014); and Chris W. Merritt, *The Coming Man from Canton: Chinese Experience in Montana, 1862–1943* (Lincoln: University of Nebraska Press, 2017). For birthright citizenship, see Martha S. Jones, *Birthright Citizens: A History of Race and Rights in Antebellum America* (Cambridge: Cambridge University Press, 2018); and Carrie Hyde, *Civic Longing: The Speculative Origins of U.S. Citizenship* (Cambridge, MA: Harvard University Press, 2018). For Yung and the CEM, see Edward J. M. Rhoads, *Stepping Forth into the World: The Chinese Educational Mission to the United States, 1872–81* (Hong Kong: Hong Kong University Press, 2011); Liel Liebovitz, *Fortunate Sons: The 120 Chinese Boys Who Came to America, Went to School, and Revolutionized an Ancient Civilization* (New York: W.W. Norton, 2011); Chih-ming Wang, *Transpacific Articulations: Student Migration and the Re-making of Asian America* (Honolulu: University of Hawai'i Press, 2013); and Clif Stratton, *Education for Empire: American Schools, Race, and the Paths of Good Citizenship* (Oakland, CA: University of California Press, 2016). For Far, see Annette White Parks, *Sui Sin Far/Edith Maude Eaton: A Literary Biography* (Urbana: University of Illinois Press, 1995); Dominika Ferens, *Edith and Winnifred Eaton: Chinatown Missions and Japanese Romances* (Urbana: University of Illinois Press, 2002); Edith Maude Eaton/Sui Sin Far, *Mrs. Spring Fragrance*, edited by Hsuan L. Hsu (Peterborough, Ontario: Broadview Press, 2011); and *Becoming Sui Sin Far: Early Fiction, Journalism, and Travel Writing by Edith Maude Eaton*, edited by Mary Chapman (Montreal: McGill-Queen's University Press, 2016).

CHAPTER 6: FEARS AND FACTS OF FILIPINO AMERICA

For the Philippine War, see M. Guerrero, *Luzon at War: Contradictions in Philippine Society, 1898–1902* (Mandaluyong City, Philippines: Anvil Publishing, 2015); Charles Quince, *Resistance to the Spanish-American and Philippine Wars: Anti-Imperialism and the Role of the Press, 1895–1902* (Jefferson, NC: McFarland, 2017); Joseph P. McCallus, *Forgotten Under a Tropical Sun: War Stories by American Veterans in the Philippines, 1898–1913*

(Kent, OH: Kent University Press, 2017). For the U.S. occupation of the Philippines, see Paul Kramer, *The Blood of Government: Race, Empire, the United States, and the Philippines* (Chapel Hill: University of North Carolina Press, 2006); Nerissa Balce, *Body Parts of Empire: Visual Abjection, Filipino Images, and the American Archive* (Ann Arbor: University of Michigan Press, 2016); Leia Castañeda Anastacio, *The Foundations of the Modern Philippine State: Imperial Rule and the American Constitutional Tradition in the Philippine Islands, 1898–1935* (New York: Cambridge University Press, 2016); Nicholas Trajano Molnar, *American Mestizos, the Philippines, and the Malleability of Race: 1898–1961* (Columbia: University of Missouri Press, 2017); and Ian Morley, *Cities and Nationhood: American Imperialism and Urban Design in the Philippines, 1898–1916* (Honolulu: University of Hawai'i Press, 2018). For Filipino Americans exclusions, see *Positively No Filipinos Allowed: Building Communities and Discourse*, edited by Antonio T. Tiongson, Jr., Edgardo V. Gutierrez, and Ricardo V. Gutierrez (Philadelphia: Temple University Press, 2006); and Rick Baldoz, *The Third Asiatic Invasion: Empire and Migration in Filipino America, 1898–1946* (New York: New York University Press, 2011).

For contexts for Louisiana Filipinos, see Donald W. Davis, *Washed Away?: The Invisible Peoples of Louisiana's Wetlands* (Lafayette, LA: University of Louisiana at Lafayette Press, 2010); David Head, *Privateers of the Americas: Spanish American Privateering from the United States in the Early Republic* (Athens: University of Georgia Press, 2015); and Joseph F. Stoltz III, *A Bloodless Victory: The Battle of New Orleans in History and Memory* (Baltimore: Johns Hopkins University Press, 2017). For early-twentieth-century Filipino histories, see Adam Lifshey, *Subversions of the American Century: Filipino Literature in Spanish and the Transpacific Transformation of the United States* (Ann Arbor: University of Michigan Press, 2016); Richard B. Meixsel, *Frustrated Ambition: General Vicente Lim and the Philippine Military Experience, 1910–1944* (Norman: University of Oklahoma Press, 2018). For the Filipino labor movement, see Craig Scharlin, *Philip Vera Cruz: A Personal History of Filipino Immigrants and the Farmworkers Movement* (Seattle: University of Washington Press, 2000); Gerald Horne, *Fighting in Paradise: Labor Unions, Racism, and Communists in the Making of Modern Hawaii* (Honolulu: University of Hawai'i Press, 2011); and Ron Chew, *Remembering Silme Domingo and Gene Viernes: The Legacy of Filipino American Labor Activism* (Seattle: University of Washington Press, 2012). For Bulosan, see *Writer in Exile/Writer in Revolt: Critical Perspectives on Carlos Bulosan*, edited by Jeffrey Arellano Cabusao (Lanham, MD: University Press of America, 2016); Vince Schleitwiler, *Strange Fruit of the Black Pacific: Imperialism's Racial Justice and Its Fugitives* (New York: New York University Press, 2017); and E. San Juan, *Carlos Bulosan: Revo-*

lutionary Filipino Writer in the United States: A Critical Appraisal (New York: Peter Lang, 2017).

CHAPTER 7: EVERYTHING JAPANESE INTERNMENT GOT WRONG

For recent histories of internment, see Anne M. Blankenship, *Christianity, Social Justice, and the Japanese American Incarceration during World War II* (Chapel Hill: University of North Carolina Press, 2016); Rachel Pistol, *Internment during the Second World War: A Comparative Study of Great Britain and the USA* (London: Bloomsbury Press, 2017); Linda L. Ivey, *Citizen Internees: A Second Look at Race and Citizenship in Japanese American Internment Camps* (Santa Barbara, CA: Praeger, 2017); and Roger W. Lotchin, *Japanese-American Relocation in World War II: A Reconsideration* (New York: Cambridge University Press, 2018). For Korematsu and legal resistance, see Roger Daniels, *The Japanese American Cases: The Rule of Law in Time of War* (Lawrence: University Press of Kansas, 2013); Erik K. Yamamoto, *Race, Rights, and Reparation: Law and the Japanese American Internment* (New York: Wolters Kluwer, 2013, 2nd edition); Lorraine K. Bannai, *Enduring Conviction: Fred Korematsu and His Quest for Justice* (Seattle: University of Washington Press, 2015); and Yamamoto, *In the Shadow of Korematsu: Democratic Liberties and National Security* (New York: Oxford University Press, 2018).

For Japanese American soldiers in WWII, see Gwenfread E. Allen, *Hawaii's War Years, 1941–1945* (Honolulu: University of Hawai'i Press, 1999 reprint); Masayo Duus, *Unlikely Liberators: The Men of the 100th and 442nd* (Honolulu: University of Hawai'i Press, 2006); Minoru Masuda, *Letters from the 442nd: The World War II Correspondence of a Japanese American Medic* (Seattle: University of Washington Press, 2008); Linda Tamura, *Nisei Soldiers Break Their Silence: Coming Home to Hood River* (Seattle: University of Washington Press, 2012); James McCaffrey, *Going for Broke: Japanese American Soldiers in the War against Nazi Germany* (Norman: University of Oklahoma Press, 2013); and Scott McGaugh, *Honor before Glory: The Epic World War II Story of the Japanese American GIs Who Rescued the Lost Battalion* (Boston: Da Capo Press, 2016). For post-internment histories, see Greg Robinson, *After Camp: Portraits in Midcentury Japanese American Life and Politics* (Berkeley: University of California Press, 2012); and Sharon Luk, *The Life of Paper: Letters and a Poetics of Living Beyond Captivity* (Oakland: University of California Press, 2018). For Kochiyama, see Diane Carol Fujino, *Heartbeat of Struggle: The Revolutionary Life of Yuri Kochiyama* (Minneapolis: University of Minnesota Press, 2005); and *Afro Asia: Revolutionary Political and Cultural Connections between African Americans and Asian Americans*, edited by Fred Ho and Bill V. Mullen (Durham: Duke University Press, 2008).

CHAPTER 8: THERE'S NOTHING
NEW ABOUT MUSLIM AMERICANS

For contemporary Islamophobia, see Arun Kundnani, *The Muslims Are Coming!: Islamophobia, Extremism, and the Domestic War on Terror* (London: Verso Books, 2014); Jeffrey L. Thomas, *Scapegoating Islam: Intolerance, Security, and the American Muslim* (Santa Barbara, CA: Praeger, 2015); Kenneth Long, *Contemporary Anti-Muslim Politics: Aggressions and Exclusions* (Lanham, MD: Lexington Books, 2017); Erik Robert Love, *Islamophobia and Racism in America* (New York: New York University Press, 2017); and Khaled A. Beydoun, *American Islamophobia: Understanding the Roots and Rise of Fear* (Oakland: University of California Press, 2018). For Muslim American responses, see Zareena Grewal, *Islam Is a Foreign Country: American Muslims and the Global Crisis of Authority* (New York: New York University Press, 2014); Ranya Idliby, *Burqas, Baseball, and Apple Pie: Being Muslim in America* (New York: Palgrave Macmillan, 2014); Nahid Afrose Kabir, *Muslim Americans: Debating the Notions of American and Un-American* (New York: Routledge, 2017); and Nadia Marzouki, *Islam, an American Religion* (New York: Columbia University Press, 2017).

For Estevanico, see Robert Goodwin, *Crossing the Continent, 1527–1540: The Story of the First African-American Explorer of the American South* (New York: Harper Books, 2008); Dennis F. Herrick, *Esteban: The African Slave Who Explored America* (Albuquerque: University of New Mexico Press, 2018). For overall Muslim American histories, see Edward E. Curtis, *Muslims in America: A Short History* (New York: Oxford University Press, 2009); Kambiz GhaneaBassiri, *A History of Islam in America: From the New World to the New World Order* (New York: Cambridge University Press, 2010); Sylviane A. Diouf, *Servants of Allah: African Muslims Enslaved in the Americas* (New York: New York University Press, 2013, 15th anniversary edition); and Jonathan Curiel, *Islam in America* (London: Tauris Books, 2015). For nineteenth-century Muslim Americans, see Omar ibn Said, *A Muslim American Slave: The Life of Omar ibn Said* (Madison: University of Wisconsin Press, 2011); and James H. Johnston, *From Slave Ship to Harvard: Yarrow Mamout and the History of an African American Family* (New York: Fordham University Press, 2012). For early-twentieth-century communities, see Gregory Orfalea, *The Arab Americans: A History* (Northampton, MA: Olive Branch Press, 2006). For an exemplary Muslim American refugee voice, see Mohammed Al Samawi, *The Fox Hunt:*

A Refugee's Memoir of Coming to America (New York: William Morrow, 2018).

CONCLUSION: THE BATTLE IN THE AGE OF TRUMP

For exclusionary responses to Obama, see Algernon Austin, *America Is Not Post-Racial: Xenophobia, Islamophobia, Racism, and the 44th President* (Santa Barbara, CA: Praeger, 2015). For the resurgence of white supremacy, see David Neiwert, *Alt-America: The Rise of the Radical Right in the Age of Trump* (London: Verso Books, 2017); Eric Arden Weed, *The Religion of White Supremacy in the United States* (Lanham, MD: Lexington Books, 2017); and Darren J. Mulloy, *Enemies of the State: The Radical Right in America from FDR to Trump* (Lanham, MD: Rowman & Littlefield, 2018). For other contemporary exclusions, see Crystal Marie Fleming, *How to Be Less Stupid about Race: On Racism, White Supremacy, and the Racial Divide* (Boston: Beacon Press, 2018); and Greg Prieto, *Immigrants under Threat: Risk and Resistance in Deportation Nation* (New York: New York University Press, 2018). And for an exemplary inclusive alternative, see Sheryll Cashin, *Loving: Interracial Intimacy in America and the Threat to White Supremacy* (Boston: Beacon Press, 2017).

Index

Yellow Peril, 11, 78; CCBA and, 79; immigrants and, 80; threats of, 76

Yen, Chang Hon, 86

About the Author

Ben Railton is professor of English studies and coordinator of American studies at Fitchburg State University in Massachusetts. He is the author of four other books, most recently *History and Hope in American Literature: Models of Critical Patriotism* (Rowman & Littlefield, 2016). He is the current president of the New England American Studies Association (NEASA), past president and current American literature director of the Northeast Modern Language Association (NeMLA), Boston chapter co-leader for the Scholars Strategy Network (SSN), and an advisor to the American Writers Museum.

Ben is constantly working to find new opportunities to share his public scholarly writing and ideas. He has written the daily AmericanStudies blog (http://americanstudier.blogspot.com) for more than eight years, writes the biweekly Considering History column for the *Saturday Evening Post* online, and has contributed public scholarly writing to *We're History*, the *HuffPost*, *The Conversation*, and many other sites. He has given public scholarly talks in spaces as diverse as New York's Museum of the Chinese in America (MOCA), the San Francisco Public Library, the Virginia Festival of the Book in Charlottesville, and Harrisburg's Midtown Scholar bookstore. He is eager to write and talk about this book, and can be contacted with any and all such opportunities at brailton@fitchburgstate.edu.